THINKING IN PRIVATE... The Present, Past and Future

POSTS of ANDREW L. STEVANS

Also by ANDREW L. STEVANS

COUNTRY LIVIN',
Two City Teens Work a Summer on the Farm

TWO YOUTH GANGS,
Growing Up Pittsburgh

PREP SCHOOL DAYS,
The Seminary at the University of Notre Dame

SOME NOTRE DAME GREATS I'VE KNOWN

ATLANTIC FLEET
A Navy Man's Story

THINKING IN PRIVATE

The Present, Past and Future

POSTS OF

ANDREW L. STEVANS

POSTS of ANDREW L. STEVANS

THINKING IN PRIVATE... The Present, Past and Future

THINKING IN PRIVATE
The Present, Past and Future
Copyright 2015

Posts of
Andrew L. Stevans

All Rights Reserved
No portion of this publication may be reproduced, stored in any electronic system, or transmitted in any form or by any means, electronic, mechanical, photocopy, recording, or otherwise, without the written permission from the author. Brief quotations may be used in literary reviews.

ISBN: 978-0-9848340-7-5
Library of Congress Control
Number (LCCN):

For Information, Contact
P.O. Box 613, Merrifield, VA 22116-0613
Amazon.com: BOOKS

Front Cover photo:
Robert Sergeant's "Finding the Nerve"
Copyright 1997: Longwood University

Printed in the USA
7290 Investment Drive, Suite B
North Charleston, SC 29418

POSTS of ANDREW L. STEVANS

THINKING IN PRIVATE… The Present, Past and Future

For Louise
*wife, mother, and a best friend
to all who meet her*

POSTS of ANDREW L. STEVANS

THINKING IN PRIVATE... The Present, Past and Future

"Our lives begin to end the day we become silent about the things that matter."

MARTIN LUTHER KING, JR

POSTS of ANDREW L. STEVANS

THINKING IN PRIVATE... The Present, Past and Future

CONTENTS

Preface... xvi

I LESSONS

Winning Achievement... 3

It's all in the Game... 5

Do Good and Prosper... 7

Behavior 101... 10

Leap of Faith... 13

Great Risks, Great Rewards... 15

Competence and Culture... 17

Encouraging Words... 19

Life Fulfillment... 21

Praise with a Purpose... 24

The "R" in Relationships... 26

Trust, the Great Motivator... 28

New Beginnings... 30

A Good Attitude & Anticipating Need... 32

How We Stay Young... 35

II PERSONAL REMEMBRANCE

Ike's Dream Generation... 37

The Parade & Carnival... 39

POSTS of ANDREW L. STEVANS

On Death and Dying... 42
Joey... 45
Tommy Boy... 48
Veterans' Day... 51
Peace Time Service... 54
One among Many... 58
Winter of Discontent...62
Writing My Way Out of a Rut... 65
Sin and Virtue... 68
Chawin' Habit... 71
A Mothers' Day Gift... 75
Really Staying in Touch... 79
The Family Health Issue... 82

III RECALLED or OVERHEARD

Critique: Criticism and Cynicism... 88
Face-To-Face... 91
Resolutions and Resolve... 95
Rude Awakening... 98
The Accelerator... 101
The Happiness Gene... 105
Internet Annoyances...108
The Youth of Today... 111

THINKING IN PRIVATE... The Present, Past and Future

The Well-Offered Toast... 113
Y2K – The Way It Was... 116
An unforgettable Personality... 118

IV HISTORY

Perseverance... 124
Northern Virginia History... 127
National Treasures... 130
The Carillons of Central New York... 133
Two Moral Leaders... 136
Gang Warfare... 140
Heroes and Hope... 143
We are One Through Humor... 145
Love and Caring... 148
Courage of Conviction... 150
Nature vs. Nurture... 152
Noblesse Oblige... 155
Ennobling Obsession... 158

V UNSOLICITED COMMENTARY

Giving Back... 164
Belief: All in the Eye of the Beholder... 168

POSTS of ANDREW L. STEVANS

Fear Tactics—the ISMs... 171

Love Thy Neighbor or else... 178

Reality Check... 181

Military Pay... 186

Congressional Retirement... 188

Decision-making under Stress... 192

Predicting Long-Term Success... 195

High Performance Cultures... 198

Cultural Hegemony... 201

Arrogance in the System... 205

A Belated Message to our Congress... 210

Pretense... 212

Gas Price Manipulation... 214

Drug Companies...216

Medical Murder?... 219

The Computer Elite... 222

THINKING IN PRIVATE... The Present, Past and Future

POSTS of ANDREW L. STEVANS

Preface

MANY OF THE "THINKING IN PRIVATE" posts originally appeared in a newsletter written for a U.S. India company headquartered in the Washington, DC area. The newsletter was sent to a dozen major U.S. cities where the company had offices--I imagined myself a syndicated writer.

The intent was to entertain as much as to evoke thought; to cause readers to collectively ponder a bit. The 250–350 word columns, short essays by any measure, became a popular read throughout the company. The column appeared in the newsletter for several years. The many selections ran the gamut on subject matter.

POSTS

When asked why the short essays are called posts, I think of all the news sources with that title--The Washington Post, the Huffington Post, The Pittsburgh Post Gazette, etc. The best answer is that each observation stands alone. In this regard they're similar to the Op-Ed pages of a newspaper rather than the related chapters found in a novel or a single subject discussion as found in most blogs. In the table-of-

THINKING IN PRIVATE... The Present, Past and Future

contents there has been an attempt to categorize the subjects into some order. I'm not sure I've succeeded.

The posts in the first three sections are short narratives about life's specifics: Love, Humor, Faith, Life and Death. Some others are categorized as "Unsolicited Commentary," broaching discussion-type news subjects—the ones we may hear about from the pundits on a daily basis. Much of the unsolicited commentary did not appear in the India U.S. newsletter.

Over the years I've recorded a few <u>Lessons</u> learned, both by me and others, with titles like: *Do Good and Prosper* and *Behavior 101*. The <u>Personal Remembrance</u> section details some of my personal experiences: *A (Halloween) Parade and Carnival,* a longer post about using a *Dot-Com Shopping Network,* and one post that appeared in the Pittsburgh Post Gazette about a teen's fascination with chewing tobacco in *Chawin Habit.*

Some of what is posted in the <u>Recalled and Overheard</u> section, we learned collectively: *The Happiness Gene*, *The Youth of Today*, *Face to Face*. The <u>History</u> section posts describe past events and people: *Perseverance, Heroes and Hope* and *Moral Leaders*.

The <u>Unsolicited Commentary</u> category, the final section, is an attempt to "bring it all out in the open", *Love They Neighbor, or else, Cultural Hegemony, Arrogance in the System*. It's possible some clarity has been brought to several

POSTS of ANDREW L. STEVANS

taboo issues that I'm not certain are considered politically correct, for example *Medical Murder?, The Drug Companies, Congressional Retirement Benefits, The Computer Elite.*

There was the question, "Do you have the right to speak for America (re: U.S. India newsletter), or, to speak at all (re: taboo subjects)?" I'll answer both questions through an early nineteenth century Frenchman's comment. Alexis de Tocqueville, in his book "Democracy in America," spoke of America as a melting pot, a blend of people and cultures. De Tocqueville concluded that a sense of community brought Americans of all walks of life together and this is what makes America great.

I hope that many of the posts will bring readers together in general agreement. Of course there are a few of the unsolicited posts that may also bring readers to full attention.

"I've always felt a deep decency in the American people and a native intelligence."— **Studs Terkel**, 1970 "Hard Times: An Oral History of the Great Depression."

THINKING IN PRIVATE... The Present, Past and Future

∞
LESSONS
∞

POSTS of ANDREW L. STEVANS

THINKING IN PRIVATE... The Present, Past and Future

Winning Achievement

FREQUENTLY, GREAT ACHIEVERS win by adhering to the three general rules of *Plan carefully, Work diligently, Achieve greatly*. Yet, some consistent achievers appear to have a secret motivating ingredient. They possess an intense "personal focus" – knowing inherently what they do best. One Olympic athlete comes to mind:

Shane Gould, the Australian 15 year-old world champion distance and sprint racer was the greatest swimmer Australia has produced and indeed the world has seen. In January 1972 she swam 100 meters in 58.5 seconds and consolidated her claim to every world's freestyle swimming record for women. As a result she has been awarded almost every known sporting trophy, both at home and abroad, which recognizes outstanding athletic achievement.

Yet Shane Gould used a two-beat kick in long-distance and sprint racing. A two-beat simply means one kick for one stroke. No one in the history of sprint racing had ever used a two-beat kick, let alone won every major event. Her kick appeared lazy in the water. Yet it worked for her. And it was something that didn't work for others. Shane Gould knew what she could do best. No one else could tell her that. She set her own goals and achieved all of them in her own way.

In team sports as in work and life, motivation and good attitude are one-on-one. We are guiding ourselves to achieve consistently.

The three great essentials to achieve anything worthwhile are common sense, hard work and stick-to-itiveness **Thomas Edison**

THINKING IN PRIVATE... The Present, Past and Future

It's all in the Game
Enjoying the Sweet Smell of Success

TOMMY HENRICH, A 1940's YANKEE baseball great, said it about baseball, but really meant it about winning and about life: "To catch the ball is sheer pleasure, but to play the ball is business." Hidden within the framework of baseball are many of the keys to success: be prepared, know the rules, play fair, be a team player, compete to win. And enjoy the win—if only for the moment.

Realizing consistent success in life appears to require similar basic ingredients. Knowledge and a honed skill are insufficient if not accompanied by commitment, cooperation, and resolve. Vince Lombardi, one of football's pre-eminent coaches, believed in savoring a win. He would remind his players, "Winning isn't everything, but wanting to win is."

Above all else, Lombardi believed in determined players who were mentally focused. He would often repeat, "Get plenty of rest; fatigue makes cowards of us all." He felt strongly that tired or overworked individuals lose their purity of purpose and cannot win consistently.

Maybe that's the beauty found in every notable success. Winning consistently demands not just a love of the game, but a purity of purpose.

With Coach Lombardi in mind, if there is an essential ingredient to success, possibly the keystone on which great successes are built, it is the benefit of mature leadership. Add an inspirational leader to a prepared team and you have the elements for winning consistently -- then, if only for the moment, relax and enjoy the sweet smell of success.

Do Good and Prosper

AN OLD FRIEND OF MINE ran across a mutual acquaintance of ours in Chicago where, years earlier, we had completed some tough systems and marketing training. He told this story:

"I was not pleased to see Sam. I remembered earlier self-indulgent, endless stories about the "three Cs": Conquests, Cars, and Cash -- his family's wealth. I was surprised when Sam suggested a quiet health bar as a place of refuge from the chill of the Chicago day. We discussed families, the kids growing up, and our careers. He questioned what had happened to the endless youth that we thought we had. Though I fought it, I started to like this man. Something had happened over the years to change his outlook.

Then, Sam told a story of an incident years earlier on an elevator in the Sears Building. He had encountered an old man who appeared drunk. They were alone, descending the many floors to the street level, below. The older man leaned slightly against the younger to keep his balance. Sam moved away. By the time they had reached street level 100 stories below, the older gentleman had explained, in a British accent, that he was sick not drunk. He asked for help getting to his car and his medication.

With the old man on his arm, Sam was forced to walk slow and take long rests. The old man mumbled incoherently. There was little talk. Strong winds off Lake Michigan tore the warmth from their bodies. After seeing the sick man to his car and helping him find and take his medication, Sam started to leave. The older gentleman stopped him with a shaky hand and paid him a compliment he never forgot, "You are a splendid human being."

"I think that earnest compliment is what transformed Sam," said my friend. "Needless to say, Sam and I departed friends."

THINKING IN PRIVATE... The Present, Past and Future

When I think back to my friend's chance meeting, I am reminded of a point Anna Quindlen, the Pulitzer Prize winning New York Times journalist, made to a group of Villanova graduates, "Get a life in which you are generous. If you do not do good, doing well will never be enough."

POSTS of ANDREW L. STEVANS

Behavior 101

IN HIGH SCHOOL we incorrectly used the word *obtuse* to describe anyone with unwelcome behavior. I learned later there are at least three levels of unacceptable behavior: *intrusive, meddlesome,* and *obstructive.* Back then, we nicknamed a sneaky school prefect "Velvet Shoe." He would appear out of nowhere, usually during an embarrassing or larcenous moment. A friend and I were caught doing 90 degree competitive pull-ups on weakened shower curtain rails. Another schoolmate was caught "borrowing" a ball point pen from the prefect's office. Velvet Shoe had a real knack for sneaking up behind us during exams. As adolescents -- had we known—some of us may have described the prefect's behavior as *intrusive*, a mild form of unacceptable behavior.

THINKING IN PRIVATE… The Present, Past and Future

Some time ago, I ran into an attorney friend who was frustrated with the law practice's meddlesome general counsel, a brilliant, somewhat addled, 85-year-old trial attorney. "The old man" as they referred to him, would interrupt indiscriminately. Once, he leaned in the door during a heated interrogatory, "Why don't you move your clients to my meeting room; it's quieter there?" Just that morning, during a tense, preliminary divorce hearing, the general counsel blurted out, "The father wants the kids, she doesn't. Case closed."

I learned later that the attorneys' office had found a solution to the general counsel's meddlesome behavior. They enlisted the elderly counsel's help in researching more difficult cases. The old man was truly trying to be of assistance, but he was obviously getting in the way.

The most adverse behavior can be labeled *malicious* or obstructive. A situation happened recently at a major corporation's Human Resource department. A new employee was caught attempting to introduce a virus into the HR department's computer system. She claimed that HR had lied to her about paying for childcare. This disgruntled employee, obviously without scruples, was fired for her *malicious* behavior.

We may have a tendency to magnify unacceptable behavior during an actual situation. I'm pretty sure my attorney friend initially viewed the elderly attorney's behavior as more obstructive than meddlesome. And I'm sure that during my high school years, most of us viewed Velvet Shoe's behavior as outright malicious. Some of us still do.

Order is never observed; it is disorder that attracts attention because it is intrusive. **Eliphas Levi** 19th century magician and author

Leap of Faith

RECENTLY THERE WAS A VIEWING among a small group: Robert Sergeant's award winning photograph of a duckling standing above turbulent waters, paused, timing its leap. The duckling was on its own. A single set of small, webbed footprints followed behind, across the broad surface of an immense concrete water break. The caption read: *Finding the Nerve*.

It didn't take much imagination to read more into the scene. The duckling's yellow-down appeared raised on-end, frozen in the *fight or flight* position. We, in the group, wondered if the young bird was trying mightily to replace its fear of the unknown with a genetically engrained faith -- its programmed instinct to jump and swim. There was no consensus among the group.

There's an old saying that faith and hope always triumph over experience. It is easy to have great faith and courage when the course is sure, the road well traveled, and those we love nearby. But, doubt, disguised as a nagging fear, emerges, as we begin a new assignment or new job, or move to a house in a new place, or make other radical changes where major decisions and those we care about are involved.

During trying times we must remember that the "faith factor" is part of the human condition, that is, to be at our very best when things seem to be at their very worst. It's there, genetically engrained or otherwise, supporting our leap into the turbulent waters.

"Feed your faith and your doubts will starve to death." **Anon**

THINKING IN PRIVATE... The Present, Past and Future

Great Risks, Great Rewards
The rest of the Story...

SUCCESSFUL RISK-TAKERS SHARE similar personal traits, among them careful planning, training, and proper execution. The sports of hot-dogging, motorcycle racing, mountain climbing and surfboarding are examples of high-demand, physical risk-taking. Peter Lowe, in his article, *Risk Is a Wonderful Thing,* says there is nothing like the endorphin rush of the near-death experience of skydiving. But Lowe is quick to emphasize that real risk-takers do not incur blind risk. They assess the potential for both gain and loss, making sure the probability of gain outweighs the possibility of loss.

Often, strong communication skills are essential in life changes, for example, starting a new business, working at home, changing careers, and, of course, proposing marriage. All involve high-demand, emotional risk-taking.

The American Society for Training and Development's (ASTD's) Bill Treasurer, author of *How to Take a Risk,* teaches that there is great emotional risk and great rewards in communicating with others openly, in a non-confrontational and honest way. Treasurer emphasizes that confrontational, dishonest or one-way communication are guaranteed deal killers.

Risk-taking has its negative side. Heavy drinking, chain-smoking, compulsive overeating and impulsive spending, in short, any risk where the probability of loss outweighs the possibility of gain is appropriately called blind risk. Those guilty of blind risk-taking must consider one additional risk – the risk of instilling an ongoing sense of fear and foreboding in those for whom they care the most.

Chance favors the prepared mind – **Louis Pasteur,** 19th century microbiologist

THINKING IN PRIVATE... The Present, Past and Future

Competence and Culture
Success Depends on Both

A PERSON'S COMPETENCE IS ESSENTIAL in the climb to success, but without understanding *culture*, and the role that culture plays in long-term success, the climb-up may suddenly become a spiraling tumble-down. Some years ago, a former learned and talented classmate did not realize that his long-term scholastic and sports success was dependent on more than his competence.

Big Bill was a phenomenal student and athlete. In the classroom he was extremely bright, and breezed through difficult math, physics, philosophy and foreign languages. His logic was impeccable, and he found great sport in arguing down instructors. On the playing field, his natural abilities won him first-team in football, basketball, and ice hockey.

Yet, Big Bill was intolerant of any team member unable to compete at his level. In intramural basketball, he often dominated the court, scoring most of the points and simply ignoring less gifted teammates. Once, in the middle of a football game, he attacked his own player. He was cunning and was not thrown out of the game, but we knew it was Big Bill at his worst.

Big Bill's attitude was at odds with school tradition, and more importantly, with some of the school's 100-year-old cultural values -- *to achieve greatly through team effort* and *to do unto others, as you would have others do unto you.* After futile counseling, he was prompted to leave the school. We heard later that advisors had attempted to explain to Big Bill that the Golden Role was a universally accepted code of conduct. But that was some cultural advice Big Bill wasn't quite ready to learn -- or to accept.

"The most difficult musical instrument to play with any enthusiasm is second fiddle. Yet without second fiddle, we have no harmony." **Anon**

THINKING IN PRIVATE… The Present, Past and Future

Encouraging Words

WHETHER DIRECTED TOWARD ADULTS or toward children, effective praise and criticism appear to follow similar rules. Research aired on TV's *20/20*, has reconfirmed that directing *praise* at an individual's actions instead of at the individual is a constructive way to encourage achievement.

Elementary school students were divided into two groups. Individuals in the first group received personal praise: "You are really smart," or "You are the best." Not only did this effusive self-esteem approach backfire – some students began treating their assignments with less interest – but the group, in general, became less effective performers.

Individuals in the second group received praise for their efforts (actions), even if they performed poorly: "Overall, that was good work," or "A lot of thought went into this." The second group not only showed scholastic improvement, their attitudes remained positive. And, most encouraging, there were requests for take-home assignments.

Some years ago, Dr. Erich Fromm, in his *I'm OK, You're OK* best seller, offered similar advice when offering *criticism*. He explained that we must direct criticism toward the individual's action/s and how the action affects us, rather than toward the individual -- always avoiding finger pointing or name-calling. An appropriate remark would be, "I was surprised at your remark..." or, "Your comment has me concerned," instead of, "You were thoughtless" or, "That was a smart remark."

Whether in complex adult relationships, or in dealing with children, we can offer effective praise or criticism by focusing on the individual's actions, and not on the individual.

"Indiscriminate approval devalues." **Kit Reed,** American author

THINKING IN PRIVATE... The Present, Past and Future

Life Fulfillment

AT FLEA MARKETS, art shows, and hobby and craft events you can often meet individuals who spent decades working another job and patiently waiting to do what their hearts really desired – their "reason for being."

In a small-group study that started back in the early 1970's, retirees from the New York Central Railroad (NYC RR) began pursuing their reasons for being. One retiree moved to a South Florida community to sell chipped ham sandwiches from a small storefront. For the residents of that area, chipped ham was something new. Over a several year period, the business became a resounding success. The man commented at his 10-year railroad-retirement reunion that he wasted 45 years on the railroad and finally found fulfillment selling ham sandwiches.

Another railroad retiree undertook the breeding of miniature horses. Over the same ten-year period he had sold many ponies; in fact enough ponies to equal his railroad retirement income several times over.

A third railroad retiree learned photography and specialized in enlarged portraits of restored steam engines pulling old-fashioned passenger cars over the mountains and through the deep valleys of Western Maryland. He realized that he had found his true calling; his income was good, his friends were many, and he would never consider doing anything else.

Is there a secret formula to realizing fulfillment in life? The publisher, (Beacon Newspapers) Stuart P. Rosenthal says the key to a happy and fulfilling life is continuing to set and pursue worthy goals, within our ability, so that we always have something to look forward to.

Why do we often wait a lifetime to pursue what will ultimately bring fulfillment doing what we love? Could it be

THINKING IN PRIVATE... The Present, Past and Future

the desire for stability during crucial family-raising years; or that, early on, we simply become distracted and do not take the time to discover and then address our true life's need.

Recognizing his raison d'être early in life, an immensely successful author spoke of having followed his life's dream. He swears that he never wrote just for the money. In his recently published book, *On Writing,* he states, "I write for fulfillment. When you do something for the joy of it, you can do it forever." His name is Stephen King.

Maybe, early on, we should consider following his example. Discover and pursue our true calling. Find something that brings us personal fulfillment and allows us to live our own life's dream.

POSTS of ANDREW L. STEVANS

Praise with a Purpose
Successful flattery has rules

IN AMERICAN LIFE the art of *flattering* is an essential part of the machinery of society. Richard Stengel's recently released book, "You're Too Kind, A Brief History of Flattery," contains a perceptive chapter called "How Dale Carnegie Won Friends and Influenced People." Stengel shows how the simplest devises of paying attention, offering appreciation, and giving small flatteries have become so engrained in our way of life that it is hard to imagine functioning without them.

Popular commentator and Washington Post columnist, Jonathan Yardley, agrees with Stengel, defining flattery as basic to life's activities: "Flattery is an exchange, at once cynical and innocent, manipulative and productive. Like the white lies that can be essential to equable human relationships, flattery is a way of moving life's business along in an efficient and relatively painless way."

THINKING IN PRIVATE... The Present, Past and Future

At its core, flattery is language that advances self-interest while at once concealing it. The ancient Greeks had a word for flattery: *demos.* Public flattery was a practice the Greeks called *demagoguery.* In ancient Rome and Egypt, for example, public flattery was a key to survival during eras of mistrustful and paranoid leaders. And during the recent Nazi Germany and Stalinist Russia eras, flattery was the only form of loyalty.

According to Stengel, who appeared on NBC *Today,* there are rules of flattery -- or its handmaiden, ingratiation: "avoid complimenting in a way that makes it appear you want a reward; make sure the compliment is plausible; praise an attribute about which the recipient is uncertain; and don't leave the impression that you are a promiscuous praiser." If you must flatter – and there are times when flattery is clearly the wisest course – then by all means do it well."

"I can live for two months on a good compliment."
Mark Twain

POSTS of ANDREW L. STEVANS

The "R" in Relationships

COLLEGE STUDENTS were asked the question, "Is Respect something that is owed, earned, or expected?" The immediate answer was, "Respect is earned". Yet respect is all three. Respect for our selves is *owed* (self respect); respect from others is *earned*; and respect toward others is *expected*.

Respect is the great definer of our humanity. But it all starts with self respect. Stephan Barboza wrote: "Self esteem blossoms or wilts with self confidence - our ability to carry out our own plans or fulfill our best intentions." We are reminded of our own fragility: "I am somebody. I may be poor, uneducated, unskilled, but I *am* somebody. Respect me. Never neglect me."

THINKING IN PRIVATE... The Present, Past and Future

Respect for ourselves breeds respect for others, without which communities become withdrawn; businesses grow mediocre, or cease to exist; cities lose their friendly glow; and nations lose their compassion - and their greatness.

As freedom binds us in our way of life, mutual respect binds us in our communities, at our work, and within our circle of family and friends.

"Respect yourself and others will respect you." **Confucius**

POSTS of ANDREW L. STEVANS

Trust, the Great Motivator

TOO OFTEN WHEN GIVEN the opportunity to lead, we treat others with less than a full vote of confidence. Ralph Waldo Emerson wrote: "Trust men and they will be true to you."

Tom Peters, of *Excellence* fame, spoke of trust in the workplace. He related a story about "old school" managers at a Maryland trucking company. Back then, it didn't matter if the manager had seven years experience and the trucker had twenty, the manager called the shots. And when a trucker didn't have the right attitude he would receive "workloads" to "straighten him out." The new CEO at the trucking company said that management was the problem. He made a few suggestions.

THINKING IN PRIVATE... The Present, Past and Future

The manager of their Canton, Ohio truck terminal decided, with some skepticism, to try out the CEO's suggestions. "I started posting productivity figures, and drew a star when they did a good job. These grown guys got excited about this. I then made keys to the terminal for the 4:00 a.m. shift. They said, 'What? You're not going to be here?' I said 'If you run into a problem, solve it. If you can't, call me. Here's my number.' From that day on attitudes changed. Productivity maintained their highest levels. The place almost ran itself!"

Trusting others inspires mutual trust. An "old school" visionary, Dwight D. Eisenhower, said it another way, "You do not lead by hitting people over the head -- that's assault, not leadership."

"If anything goes bad, I did it. If anything goes real good, then we did it." **Bear Bryant,** Former Head Coach, University of Alabama

POSTS of ANDREW L. STEVANS

New Beginnings
Achieving Consistently

MUCH CAN BE LEARNED about high-performance from the Olympic Creed:

> "The most important thing in the Olympic Games is not to win, but to participate, just as the most important thing in life is not the triumph, but the struggle. The essential thing is not to have conquered, but to have fought well."

It is possible to apply the Olympic Creed to a philosophy for daily living. Some examples follow.

At the individual level, successful *participation* requires thorough preparation (training). *The struggle* is found in developing and maintaining good work habits. *Fighting*

THINKING IN PRIVATE… The Present, Past and Future

well means diligently executing our daily schedules in order to realize all of our personal and career objectives.

Within groups, for those with leadership roles, *participation* translates into dispelling others' fears and earning their trust. *The struggle* is in consistently leading by good example. *Fighting well* means to motivate more and manage less.

Whether our involvement is in Olympic play or in day-to-day living, holding fast to our basic beliefs and to a code of conduct promises continued success. As examples, effective *participation* may require that we volunteer personal time in our communities. *Our struggle* may be in showing patience and fairness, regardless of outside pressures. And *fighting well* may require advocating tolerance for others' opinions and showing respect for the individual.

"The important things are belief in ourselves, a strong work-ethic, and realizing the power of teamwork." **Bob Mathias**, twice Olympic Decathlon Gold Medalist.

A Good Attitude & Anticipating Need
The Two Golden Gifts

IN ADDITION TO A GOOD EDUCATION and possessing the organization skills and personal discipline that experience often provides, there appear to be two major requirements to realize success in any endeavor: a steady personality, that is, the ability to get along with most people (team play), and the ability to anticipate others' needs and react appropriately to address those needs (team work).

A GOOD ATTITUDE—(TEAM PLAY)... The way we present ourselves as we speak reflects our attitude. Only recently has the science of kinesics (the study of body language) discovered that how we use our bodies while speaking, such as facial expressions, posture and gestures, has

THINKING IN PRIVATE... The Present, Past and Future

its own grammar, and comprises 90% or more of our communications.

During WW II President Delano Roosevelt inspired the free world with his flamboyant and optimistic smile, holding in his clenched teeth a cigarette holder angled upward. Few people cared that he was paralyzed from the waist down. Roosevelt's confident smile and irrepressible can-do attitude served him well during his 12 years in the White House.

ANTICIPATING NEED—(TEAM WORK)... The following vignette describes this concept perfectly. Some years ago the family had moved from the Finger Lakes region of New York to Northern Virginia. A neighbor introduced her young son, Eric, to the family. Eric's father was an apartment building maintenance engineer. Eric, all of four years old, accompanied his father on minor repair efforts around the apartment complex. This youngster possessed, or had developed at a young age, an inborn sense of anticipating need. One day, as I adjusted the grass cutter height and was reaching for my pliers, little Eric already had the pliers in hand. Initially, I thought this was a simple coincidence. Later, when I reached for the screwdriver or the hammer, Eric had these ready as well. Little Eric convinced me that the gift of anticipating another's needs, that is, being a team player, can happen early in life.

Tact and staying power during problem solving efforts increase our value in a team endeavor. But when combined with proper attitude and an ability to anticipate others' needs we are guaranteed a place on any team and within any organization. These two qualities give us value not only in our work group, but also in our circle of family and friends.

THINKING IN PRIVATE… The Present, Past and Future

How We Stay Young

WHAT FOLLOWS IS A RECIPE for those seeking to maintain a youthful outlook.

--Keep only cheerful friends

--Surround ourselves with what we love

--Laugh often

--Tears happen, endure, grieve and move on

--Learn all that we can

--Enjoy the simple things

--Cherish your health

--Show those we love that we truly love them

   (Do so at every opportunity)

--Enjoy the life we have, but continue to dream

"Let us endeavor to so live that when we come to die even the undertaker will be sorry." **Mark Twain**

POSTS of ANDREW L. STEVANS

∞
PERSONAL REMEMBRANCE
∞

THINKING IN PRIVATE... The Present, Past and Future

Ike's Dream Generation
Reflections on a college reunion

AMERICA HAS ATTEMPTED TO DEFINE its generational differences by exercising the great American tradition of "labeling." Edward Gubman, author of "The Talent Solution," labels Americans born before 1946 as the *Ike Generation*. He describes *Ikes* as the generation that achieves their dreams through hard work.

One hard working group of Ikes, 12 of us in total, recently had a reunion. Two things quickly became apparent. First, we appeared a bit past our prime and, as the Levi's ad says, we were a "skosh bigger" in the wrong places. Second, we were gray or silver-haired, retired "looking," and appeared to fit a recently coined term "young seniors."

One member of the group is a photographer of some repute, a successful recording artist and a nationally recognized, award winning educator. Another taught for many years at the University of Paris, and traveled Europe as a bilingual resident. There were a published author and columnist, a computer guru who is a nationwide chain-store consultant, and a youth-gang hero who, for 17 years, has led many of his "gangsters" out of the ghetto. A recent movie script has been drafted telling of his life, his sacrifices, his love and his heroic attempts to serve the youth of the Cabrini district in Chicago.

This man is also an accomplished artist as was another member of the group who currently runs the university's art center. Notable were the number who have shared their professional knowledge in the classroom, instructing both youth and adult learners.

The reunion was a proud and humbling experience. It was the rediscovery of a small, highly successful fragment of my generation. But, more than that, it is a group that I can truly call my lifelong friends. As "young seniors," we hold the promise of many more years ahead to achieve our dreams and help better the lives of those nearest and dearest to us.

"If you won't plow in the cold, you won't eat at the harvest."
Proverbs 20: 4

THINKING IN PRIVATE... The Present, Past and Future

The Parade and Carnival
A Haunting Memory

AS YOUNG TEENAGERS, my friends and I became involved in some unlikely situations. In retrospect, we may have provoked some others. One example comes to mind.

During a particularly warm October, on the evening of the local Halloween parade, a carnival had set up in town. We planned to enter the parade competition. If any of us won, we would spend the money on carnival rides.

Two friends in our group put on masks and climbed into an extra-large clown outfit to become the "Double-Clowns." During the parade, they perfected walking in unison. The parade leaders required a close, fast moving formation in order to keep non-costumed kids from crashing the parade.

More than a few times over the half-mile parade route, the Double-Clowns made their mistake and fell down, causing other costumed figures to fall on top of them. Since many of the victims in the pile-ups were teenaged girls, the two boys viewed this as an acceptable outcome.

Witnessing the pile-ups, the parade leaders apologized to the two boys for the close formation. Later, the parade judges awarded the first prize of ten dollars to the Double-Clowns. Since there were two first place winners, the sponsors provided another ten-dollar award.

With some of us still in our costumes, we rode several of the carnival rides, later walking over to the Ferris wheel. We must have looked a sight: a pirate, a skeleton, a painted Indian, and two of us carrying a large clown costume. The Ferris wheel operator, a tall, red-faced fellow, demonstrated an uncanny knack for ducking under the Ferris wheel seats. He saw us watching as he shoved his head in and under each approaching seat, paused grinning, and pulled his head out. He made his mistake. He kept taking tickets and loading up the

THINKING IN PRIVATE... The Present, Past and Future

Ferris wheel, trying to fake it for a period of time; his face a pale mask.

    We saw how wicked the hit was. A seat had raked his neck and head. We walked away thinking that maybe we were the ones keeping him there.

POSTS of ANDREW L. STEVANS

On Death and Dying
Significant others

DURING OUR TEENAGE YEARS, some of us boys worked on farms in the summer and, in the fall, on school weekends. I recall the feast of St. Francis of Assisi, when priests from local parishes made the rounds of the farms and blessed the animals. Back then, we boys dismissed animal death as *farm death.* I felt that way until I was responsible for the death of an old farm dog.

Later, as an adult, I met a mischievous stray cat that kept showing up on the back porch. For a while we fed the cat, then sheltered her, and finally gave her a name. A few years later, she developed a tooth abscess and died from related complications. Somehow, that cat managed to leave a large hole in the family. To this day I miss both of these animals and still share stories of their unique character traits with family. I think that the deaths of pets help prepare us for the passing of family members and friends. An acquaintance brought this reality into focus recently.

During my late evening winter jaunts, a neighbor who had no local family ties confided that his wife had developed a terminal cancer. He explained that he had begun attending grieving sessions where he met with strangers on a regular basis to share his pain and to grieve openly. He said his family, all elderly, responded by phone but was unable to make the trip to visit him and his wife. We spoke for some time about many things. I hoped that I had provided him some comfort during his terrible ordeal. His death followed shortly after his spouse died.

More recently, I sent an article to my alumni group. The article announced the death of a life-long dear friend whom we all knew well. There was an immediate response-- an outpouring of concern and comments about their own serious family illnesses. I was surprised to hear such personal

POSTS of ANDREW L. STEVANS

information from our group who typically email trivia and avoid discussing our personal or families' health. In some way the article had provided a forum for venting on death and dying. I now realize that sharing the pain with others really does help to relieve the stress of great loss.

My father died recently. How consoling it is to find solace among those we've shared our lives with, and who accept and understand us.

"The only truly dead are those who have been forgotten." **Old saying**

SPECIAL NOTE Professor Tom Merluzzi, director of Notre Dame's Psycho-Oncology Research Lab, studies coping processes in cancer patients and survivors and has created the Cancer Behavior Inventory (CBI), a measure which is used worldwide. He believes if we can study how some cancer patients cope well, we can develop better care for those who struggle. His hope is that someday psychological treatment will be offered alongside chemotherapy and radiation.

THINKING IN PRIVATE... The Present, Past and Future

Joey

THERE ARE TIMES WHEN THE SIMPLEST of events call all of one's human motivations into question. I met Joey while responding to a commotion on the sidewalk near our home. Neighborhood kids of all ages surrounded the wheelchair-bound nine-year-old. He had finger puppets that he manipulated with great dexterity, all the while providing hilarious dialogue. After the show I asked Joey how he managed his wonderful act. Glancing up with penetrating dark eyes and a crooked smile, he held up a puppet and said, "I just keep them dancing." He exited down the sidewalk, his wheelchair squeaking.

Some months later while visiting the Children's Hospital I met Joey once again. He was entertaining a group of young patients with puppets and a dialogue as comical as ever. A nurse confided that Joey had a habit of seeking out the sickest or most depressed children. "He is our little angel." I noticed Joey's right hand was not functioning well, his chest was wrapped in gauze under his hospital gown, and his shoulders were slightly hunched.

Later that morning upon stepping off a hospital elevator, I heard loud adult laughter and observed Joey entertaining a group of doctors and technical staff from the hall through a conference room window. Joey exited down the corridor. After each wheelchair squeak he glanced back at us with a pained smile. "That youngster is an old soul," one staff member commented.

A long buried memory transformed the scene. Joey's blue hospital gown became a faded blue sari; his arched back became that of a small, stooped woman. Mother Teresa made a brief statement to the awed assembly, "We can do no great things; only small things with great love."

The memory cleared. I again saw little Joey with the crooked smile and large eyes that stared through me. He waved back at us as children started to gather around him.

Keep them dancing, Joey. Keep them dancing!

THINKING IN PRIVATE… The Present, Past and Future

POSTS of ANDREW L. STEVANS

Tommy Boy

IN THE EARLY 1990's, Simon & Schuster Publishers persuaded M. Scott Peck, the noted psychiatrist and best selling author of *The Road Less Traveled,* to write a book on evil. Surprisingly, Dr. Peck titled the book *People of the Lie,* explaining that lying was a key element of evil. While reading the book, I thought of Tommy, a boyhood friend, and hoped that Scott Peck wasn't implying that all liars are evil.

Without noticeable effort Tommy could create some preposterous, on the spot exaggerations or outright lies about the events of the day. His creative tall-tale telling and quick Irish wit endeared him to everyone he met. We once asked his cousin why he lied so much. She replied in her best Irish brogue: "Early in life Tommy boy kissed the Blarney Stone."

Following military service and college, Tommy found computer work at a hometown bank. Tommy's yarns and popularity reached new levels. He was a dedicated worker, respected by bank management, and moved quickly into upper management positions. I had moved from the area but stayed in touch with Tommy.

On a visit back home several years ago, I spoke with Tommy for the last time. He explained that he had lung cancer. I didn't know whether to believe him, but accepted that he wouldn't kid about such a serious matter. Shortly afterwards I heard from friends that Tommy had passed away quietly in his sleep. I had lost a dear friend.

Recently, I ran into an acquaintance from years earlier. He had worked with Tommy at the bank. He made a comment about Tommy's management style: "Anything Tommy promised he delivered on. Everyone wanted to work for that guy. We all miss Tommy and his outrageous lies." Had M. Scott Peck known Tommy, I think that he would have called him a good liar, not an evil one. He would have missed Tommy, too.

"Baloney is an unvarnished lie, blarney is the varnished truth." **Irish humor**

THINKING IN PRIVATE... The Present, Past and Future

Veteran's Day

A Day of Remembrance

SOME TIME BACK, when the nation prepared for another war, a group of us veterans sat around a table outside a local restaurant. A jogger approached. His shorts were stripped white and red; his buttocks flashed stars on blue. We took exception to the idea of the U. S. Flag being represented on a sweaty, tight-fitting pair of runner's shorts. A few of us started to get up to bar his approach. The jogger was giving us a "What's your problem?" look, when a young man, exiting the local grocery store, accidentally knocked him down, strewing groceries all over the side walk. The jogger arose painfully, slipping on ripped bags and spilled vegetable oil. He disappeared around the building.

POSTS of ANDREW L. STEVANS

We gladly helped pick up the young man's groceries and clean up the mess. One veteran asked him if he was ready to fight for his country--again. We all laughed. He seemed confused. He started off quickly on dirty tennis shoes, yelling a friend. "You can thank us later," one of us said. "Oh. Yeah," was his blank-faced reply. He hunched up his boxed groceries and extended a limp hand.

We returned to our chairs to discuss near wars and wars of the recent past: the Suez crises, the Iraq war, the Lebanon Uprising, the Liberty Incident – the "cold" war. We recalled the stress on the country--the anxiety among military families that the threat of another war evokes.

Perhaps war has a better effect than the horror of thinning a generation. At such times the living cherish life and love and the moment.

War teaches instant fear, and respect and responsibility. During these stressful times, God lives; smiles are returned with smiles; thanks is gladly given--and the flag waves free.

THINKING IN PRIVATE... The Present, Past and Future

POSTS of ANDREW L. STEVANS

Peace Time Service?

U.S. Navy: 1955-1961:

FEW FAMILIES REALIZE the inherent danger to family members serving in the "peacetime" armed forces. I recall a few crises faced by my squadron of eight destroyers and the U.S.S. Hank, a destroyer from a sister squadron. The incidents related occurred during my service in the Atlantic Fleet and involved hundreds of men in our squadron and, during the Suez Crisis, many thousands of personnel as well as a few hundred ships. Navy War Condition III requires a 24 hour, full-ship's alert, that is, manned weapons stations, half the ship on duty around the clock (known as port and starboard watch) and complete black-out conditions-- sometimes with a single search-light on each ship's largest flag.

THINKING IN PRIVATE... The Present, Past and Future

--The Suez Canal Crisis (War Condition III)... During the month of December 1957, I was a young petty officer aboard a 300-man Navy destroyer, the USS Heermann. A massive U.S. Sixth Fleet war maneuver was in progress off the coast of France. The entire U.S. fleet, an armada that covered the sea from horizon to horizon, had been placed on War Condition III watch.

The British, French and Israeli forces were about to go to war with Egypt to halt their blockage of the Suez Canal. The U.S. Sixth Fleet was ordered to surround British and French war ships headed to the Suez area, to challenge them, but to not allow them out of our circle of war ships. At night, each American ship flew its largest ensign (flag). All main deck lights aboard ships were ordered extinguished except for a search light, lighting up each ship's American flag. Finally, the British and French returned to their respective home ports.

All Anglo-French forces withdrew before the end of the year, but Israel, with its borders next to Egypt's, remained until March 1958, prolonging the crisis. In April 1958, the Suez Canal was reopened to shipping.

POSTS of ANDREW L. STEVANS

--The Lebanon Uprising (War Condition III)... The USS Heerman, and several other ships in our eight destroyer squadron, transported U.S. Marines to secure the Lebanon airport. The July 1958 *Lebanon Crisis* as it was later referred to, was a Lebanese political crisis caused by both political and religious tensions in the country that included our intervention. The intervention lasted three months until President Camille Chamoun, who had requested the American assistance, completed his term as president of Lebanon. American and Lebanese government forces successfully occupied the port and international airport of Beirut. In October with the crisis over, the United States war ships withdrew.

--USS Hank Incident... Off Cape Hatteras, NC, November 1958. In Norfolk, Virginia, I was assigned to the USS Hank DD 702, for transport to Golfe Juan, France to report for cruiser duty aboard the USS Newport News, CA 148. A few days out of Norfolk heavy seas damaged the Hank, the waves beating against the main deck's protected walkway. Railroad ties were used to force the walkway open and keep the corridor from complete collapse. The Hank suffered a 35+

THINKING IN PRIVATE... The Present, Past and Future

degree list. This would have put the Hank on its side but for the 03 level Mk 56 gun director. The director was engineered to fall into the sea at a 35 degree list. This saved the Hank and allowed the battered ship to limp back to Norfolk for repairs.

There were always ways to relieve tension during high stress times. Daily, during the pre-Christmas Suez Crises, a dozen or more of enlisted personnel including several officers assembled in a forward gun mount and practiced four-part Christmas carols. In black-out conditions, some of us in Fox Division congregated below decks to play cards, trade jokes and tell sea stories, awaiting our port and starboard, 12 hour watch on the ship's bridge.

"The worst is not always certain but it's very likely." **French Proverb**

One among Many

Moving On in order to Move Up

I'M PRETTY SURE THE EARLY explorers and inventors had many critics as well as a large cheering section. And I'm fairly sure that many of these followers were able to provide their versions of what the great ones "should be doing" or "should have done."

In his book "Mandate for Change," Eisenhower made the comment that human nature has remained the same throughout history. Today's "wanna-bes" continue to support or slam the accomplishments of the Steve Jobs and Bill Gates, pro sports figures, our politicians—they're a talkative bunch and the list is long. Our current day journeymen critics can be found filling the seats of bars, alehouses and beer gardens around the world.

THINKING IN PRIVATE... The Present, Past and Future

Some years ago, my youngest son was contemplating a move into a military career.

"I talked it over with my friends," he explained. "I'm turning 21 and haven't found my niche, yet." The Air Force is willing to train me in air-traffic control." I listened with some interest--even though I'm a Navy guy, myself.

"Who did you talk to?" I asked since I knew his friends from the neighborhood. Then I heard that he'd presented his situation to an older, ex-Marine friend who was his evening manager at a local restaurant. I immediately felt some anxiety.

"I know your friend means well and wouldn't want to hurt your feelings by disagreeing with you."

"Well dad, he suggested I go into the marines."

I was taken back. I didn't want to damn his friend, yet I felt my blood pressure rising. My son also explained that he had his critics. One of his friends said that the times were perilous and war could happen at any time. Another urged him to stick around home.

"You'll find the right opportunity, soon," he assured him, while tossing back another beer.

POSTS of ANDREW L. STEVANS

In a fortunate moment, I said the right thing. I urged my son to learn some skill in the military that would continue to provide him a decent living when he re-entered civilian life. I explained that no one could predict when war would break out. I emphasized my own post Navy experience; how surprisingly little had changed among several of my friends when I had returned home—discussing their high-school girl friends, the endless sports talk. A major difference was that I had learned more than a little about electronics and computers during my Navy hitch, and was immediately employed into a local computer group, earning a decent income.

The other day, my son, now a superintendent of air traffic control and contemplating his retirement from the Air Force, reminded me of my statement so many years earlier.

"Do you know, dad, I still find a few of my school buddies just hanging out, living for the Friday night Happy Hours. I've run into them over the years and they're pretty savvy guys. They can discuss politics, smart phones, apps, sports and other interesting things. But, like you told me, they still reminisce about old high-school sweethearts and re-live

THINKING IN PRIVATE... The Present, Past and Future

the great football wins, back when they played the game." He paused for a minute

"But, you didn't warn me about one thing."

I'm sure I looked concerned.

"Now, they expect me to pick up the tab for their brews."

POSTS of ANDREW L. STEVANS

Winter of Discontent

Finding new meaning in giving

IT WAS A FEW DAYS BEFORE CHRISTMAS. As I walked to my car in a blowing rain and snow storm, a ragged, bedraggled soul interrupted my last minute shopping as I walked to my car. I listened to her story. She asked for bus money to return home to her children in a nearby town. She wished me happy holidays. Her tired smile returned me to reality.

In every city and town north of Tampa, from late September through early May, there are homeless individuals suffering from cold and hunger. Many also suffer year-round from the feelings of loneliness and alienation.

Former President Jimmy Carter said recently that, during his tenure in office, there were a few hundred homeless

THINKING IN PRIVATE... The Present, Past and Future

in Atlanta. It has now grown to thousands, and many of these are dislocated families. Street people, most just like you and me -- men, women, and a growing number of young homeless families -- face an endless winter of discontent, and hold absolutely no hope for tomorrow.

The risk of confrontation in the streets is real, but our genuine interest in getting to know someone cut off from society can be, in and of itself, supremely effective. For ten years during the early eighties through the mid-nineties, Lee Stringer, the acclaimed author of "Grand Central Winter," lived in the streets of New York City. He was a homeless, hooked-on-heroine junkie. "Public Policy," he later wrote, "is never the real issue. The real issue is the hearts of men. Money helps, but isolation and disenfranchisement take the greatest toll on people in the streets."

Anna Quinlen, Pulitzer Prize winning New York Times journalist, addressed a Villanova graduating class, "If we do not try to do good, doing well will never be enough." She went on to describe her futile efforts to help an alcoholic living on the streets near Coney Island. She decided to listen to his story and agree with his observation that the ocean view was inspiring. She left, inspired by him.

    Good will and a spirit of giving is important in providing the homeless food, clothing, and shelter. Yet, we all lose in the sterile environment of giving things, and not lending an ear to those who ache for the human touch. And all of us are the poorer for it.

"When it comes to giving, some people will stop at nothing."
Jimmy Carter

THINKING IN PRIVATE... The Present, Past and Future

Writing My Way Out of a Rut

IN THE MID-NINETIES my contract work in the Washington DC area disappeared. Month after month I existed on denial and a few hours' sleep each night.

Following one particularly bad week during the year-end holidays, I read an article about writing ones way out of depression. The article went on to say that recording one's personal life-experiences was a cheap form of psycho-analysis.

I began writing short essays about a summer, during my early teens, working—and getting in and out of trouble--on a farm south of Pittsburgh, Pennsylvania, my old home town.

The farm stories became a book. I titled the book "COUNTRY LIVIN' *Two City Teens Work a Summer on the Farm.*" The stories seemed to take on a life of their own and became my new obsession, replacing the gnawing fear and worry of the failing business.

By pure luck—possibly in answer to fervent prayer--I ran into a former school friend whose sister was editor for the *Pittsburgh Magazine*. After reviewing the manuscript, the sister thought the stories publishable and suggested I submit them to the Pittsburgh Post Gazette.

Over the next 12 months, many of the vignettes appeared in the Post Gazette's Sunday Metro section. The farm families were surprised to see their names in print, and to read about events that happened so many years earlier. Some of the families contacted me and I sent additional unpublished stories. The following year, I visited the farms with my wife. Old friendships were rekindled.

My fifteen minutes of writing fame relieved the terrible stress that had affected my work and my personal relationships. I discovered a way to work smarter and was

THINKING IN PRIVATE... The Present, Past and Future

contracted, then hired into a fast growing local company. I've not been in denial or suffered a bout of depression since.

"A man should strive to get into accord with his complexes; they are legitimately what direct his conduct in the world."
Sigmund Freud

POSTS of ANDREW L. STEVANS

Sin and Virtue

IN BEN FRANKLIN'S "Book of Virtues," he provides a character building exercise that can be followed by any generation. Each month, Ben Franklin would select and concentrate on one of his listed 13 virtues, practicing Humility or Moderation or Sincerity—and thus growing his personal character a little at a time.

As a senior-year student, attending Holy Cross Seminary at the University of Notre Dame, I had selected as my spiritual advisor (and, in my mind, as confidant) Father Leonard Banas, CSC. At that time, Father Len was a Holy Cross resident Priest, a Notre Dame classical language expert, a fine athlete and a shining example for a strong-willed character like me.

THINKING IN PRIVATE... The Present, Past and Future

Father Len, acting as my spiritual coach and advisor, provided me a monthly objective. For example, one month my objective was to build "Tolerance." Father provided synonyms for tolerance that were easy to relate to, such as "Charity, Mercy." For the next 30 days, I would attempt to incorporate tolerance into my daily living.

This approach managed to keep me busy for a month, and at month-end I would meet with Father Len to provide him examples of my progress. I was then provided a new spiritual objective for the next month. I discovered later that Father's approach to spiritual direction was similar to Ben Franklin's approach to character building. I attribute Father Len's spiritual coaching to a list I later constructed of the Seven Deadly Sins and the Seven Cardinal Virtues.

SEVEN DEADLY SINS

P R I D E (Conceit, Inordinate Self-esteem)

L U S T (Immoral, Intense & Excessive Sexual Desire)

A NGER (Fury, Uncontrolled Temper)

G L U T T O N Y (Indulgence, Excessive Eating)

POSTS of ANDREW L. STEVANS

U S U R Y (Avarice, ~Greed)
E N V Y (Jealousy, Resentment)
S L O T H (Apathy, Laziness)

SEVEN PERSONAL VIRTUES
V E R A C I T Y (Honesty, Devotion to the Truth)
I N T E G R I T Y (Decency, Moral Character)
R E S P E C T (Value, Worthy of Esteem)
T O L E R A N C E (Forbearance, Patience)
U N D E R S T A N D I N G (Considerate, Insightful)
E M P A T H Y (Compassion, Sensitivity)
S E L F – C O N T R O L (Restraint, Self-Discipline)

To this day I consider Father Len Banas, (a.k.a. "The Pastor of Elkhart County, Indiana") my spiritual advisor. I'm not so sure he continues to assume this responsibility.

Chawin' Habit

Nipped in the Taste Bud

FOR A 13 YEAR-OLD, CITY OF PITTSBURGH teen, an offer to work on Merle's farm for the summer brought on a feeling of pure joy and exhilaration. Jim, an older brother's friend, had worked on the farm the summer before. But his family was buying a farm in the next county, so Jim needed someone to "learn the ropes" on Merle's farm, and assume his responsibilities. I want to use the word "responsibilities" carefully here. Sure, there was work, but…

It was a few days after Jim and my tomato throwing war that we joined a large group of farmers from neighboring farms, gathered to help with threshing wheat on a section of Ray's, Merle's brother's farm.

POSTS of ANDREW L. STEVANS

Mowing machines cut the wheat grass, then straightened and tied the straw into armful-size bundles. The bundles or "shocks" as we called them were immediately collected by hand. Five were placed on end in a circle with a sixth spread over the top as a moisture barrier.

Shocking wheat is man's work. It's a ritual, starting at sunup, stopping for lunch in the grand style of farm lunches and continuing until sunset.

The crew, comprised of local farmers from a farm co-op (everybody pitched in to help each farmer mow and thresh their farm) was grateful for all the help. And everybody was in fine spirits.

While we worked, the farmers' wives were busy at the house preparing a grand luncheon feast. But I wouldn't be eating lunch that day. I was destined to learn a valuable lesson.

One of the crew was a farmer who looked Chinese. I watched as he chewed tobacco then spit it out. I wondered why he had to get rid of it so often. Finally, I asked him.

"Well, it tastes like chocolate after you chew it awhile," he said pensively. "You spit very far and hit anything you aim at." I'm sure he watched my eyes light up as he pinged a few rails.

I memorized the easy way his fingers grasped and measured the chaw. I wanted to know all the moves.

I took a fresh wad. He showed me how to hold it in my cheek, up high. I didn't like the sharp tobacco taste, but the thought of long spits and deadly accuracy drove me on.

We kept moving and shocking. It was hot. Everyone was shirtless as we worked across the field. The tobacco became separated and moist in my mouth. Its juice thinned the saliva. I could spit long trails.

But this wasn't my game. The stuff stung my tongue. Forgetting, I swallowed it. My stomach burned with nausea.

The farmer knew I was sick. He saw me stagger.

"Are you dizzy?" he asked.

"Yes," I answered, meekly. "I swallowed the wad, and I'm as sick as a dog."

"You spit with it, you don't eat it," he explained. He looked pensive again. "Do you want some more?" he asked.

"No," I said, becoming sicker at the thought of it.

POSTS of ANDREW L. STEVANS

My habit was cured before it ever started.

"Good judgment comes from experience. Experience comes from bad judgment." **Mark Twain**

THINKING IN PRIVATE... The Present, Past and Future

A Mothers' Day Gift
Sometimes, Dot-Com Mail Order Doesn't Work

I DIDN'T KNOW AT THE TIME, but the nightmare started on April 16. The dot-com e-mail advertisement read: "Surprise mom with this lovely ring, aglow with flowing waves of gold." A photo of a gold band containing family names and birthstones was prominently displayed. There was room on the ring for four names and four gemstones, perfect for our three, now grown, children's names and my own.

In mid-April I ordered the ring and received an e-mail confirmation. In Late April, I received another e-mail with a shipping number. The following day, April 29, my bank account was charged for the ring. I'm lucky to have a Post Office Box in a major USPS facility. It's open on Sundays.

Ten days into May—on Mothers' Day, the ring finally

arrived. It was in a shipping container half as big as a shoebox. The Postmarked mailing-strip said: "El Paso April 30." I wondered if the ring had been lost in the holiday mails.

Now, the rest of the story...

Mother's Day was quickly approaching. Having not received the ring, I e-mailed a query on May 6, and again on May 8. I thought, "If the mailed ring was sent by Fed Ex or UPS, it will not be delivered to a U.S. Post Office mail box."

Finally, on May 9, I called the store's dot-com 800-number and volunteered a question: "Could the ring have been sent Parcel Post, the slowest (and cheapest) way to mail via USPS?" The kind but tired Customer Service lady assured me that the order was sent via U.S. Mail. She did not know if it was sent Parcel Post. She confirmed an April 28 shipping date. I verified the name and shipping address.

My second e-mail was answered on Saturday, May 10. It was titled: "Dear Ms. Harden," even though my name and mailing address were at the bottom of the e-mail. The rest of the form message mentioned concern, sincere apologies and

THINKING IN PRIVATE... The Present, Past and Future

the inconvenience. It fell on dead ears. The e-mail ended, "We look forward to *see* you soon at our store."

Following a Mothers' Day breakfast, my wife, daughter and I proceeded to make one final check at the Main Post Office. The ring had arrived! I carefully opened the shipping box and found a white cardboard container that yielded a small silver vase and a stemmed red silk rose. An enclosed "special" Mothers Day card lauded the jewelry as well as the silk rose and the "gleaming" vase. Among the Shipment Summary page, The Jewelry Repair page, and the Return *Parcel Post* page, we discovered a clear plastic envelope with a small blue velvet pull-string bag. Inside the bag was the coveted ring, wrapped in tissue paper. As my wife unwrapped the tight strands of tissue, my daughter and I searched fruitlessly for the promised personal message that was to read, "*To a dedicated wife and mom. Love*," followed by my name and the three children's.

My wife's eyes squinted to see the ring's inscriptions. Her attempts to show surprise and appreciation became a look of concern. I offered my sincere apologies for the tiny replica of the advertised ring. "It's a $250 Pinky-ring!" my daughter complained. My wife had her electronics inspector's 10X magnifying scope -- a retirement gift from her former employer -- trained on the ring to view the inscriptions. She commented that the names were well done, but too small to see with the naked eye. I quietly returned the rose, vase and card, and the velvet bag with ring to the mailing carton for a return and refund from the dot-com store.

Five days more and the dot-com ring order would have taken one-full month to arrive. I calculated that I had spent – wasted – a minimum of four hours during that one-month waiting period. This included several trips to the post-office, the e-mails and follow-up phone call, and returning the ring. Using that same amount of time and effort, the family could have scoured a dozen stores and jewelry outlets, and even gone to lunch, and enjoyed a much better time finding a similar gift.

In that regard my personal advice, if you are contemplating ordering jewelry via the Internet – don't. My dot-com ring shopping days are over– no apologies.

THINKING IN PRIVATE... The Present, Past and Future

Really Staying in Touch

Communications and Aging

NONE OF US RETIRED GUYS, whether relatives or alumni or old work associates or friends really remain in touch. By "really," I mean the few retired guys with computer skills, who think they're communicating, typically don't open up about themselves. We're all hundreds of miles from each other and the poorer for it. Of course, I get plenty of emails: cut-and-paste jokes, cartoons, etc. There's little "here's what's going on in my life" type stuff.

The women also send these kinds of emails, typically with more emphasis on the three "Ps" prayers, poems and pictures. But the women will also occasionally email about serious medical problems and other family matters: "Our youngest is leaving for college. I didn't think we'd feel like empty nesters, but here we are."

Other than the few and far between proud travel commentaries and jpg photos of their trips, it's my experience that the guys seldom disclose anything about their life's journeys, incidents in their daily living, or their health and other age related experiences.

Over the years, I would receive cards from family and friends for birthdays, anniversaries, Christmases, etc. And it was pretty obvious that the wives—often sisters'-in-law--wrote short messages, and even addressed the envelopes.

It used to take me off guard, still does, when one of the guys sends a brief comment in a greeting card saying, "Enjoy your Christmas," or, "Have a great birthday," or "Don't drink too much in the New Year," or, "Sorry to hear you're dead!"
I would like to say, "C'mon gentlemen. You're retired now. There's no excuse for not writing."

My sister is one of six children, the fourth child among us five boys. For many years Sis has been an extremely busy, now "semi-retired", director of teaching nurses in Central

THINKING IN PRIVATE... The Present, Past and Future

Florida. She remains busy with her job, busier than most of the younger people she works with. Sure, she's guilty of sending the "three Ps", but Sis has always managed to find time to send an annual letter—a complete update on her family, life events--some good news some bad. Sis has been doing this since the 1970s!

Sure, she brags a little in her letters and emails, writes about her three kids' their school events, and, in later correspondence, her kids' marriages and her grandkids. But Sis would include humorous incidents that happened during the year. I've saved most of her Christmas letters in a binder. Occasionally, I'll re-read and savor some of them; even saved and re-read some of her over-the-years emails. I treasure the fact that, over this long period of time, Sis has taken the time to really stay in touch.

"We're the most aggressively inarticulate generation to come along since, you know, a long time ago!" **Taylor Mali**, American author, teacher, actor

POSTS of ANDREW L. STEVANS

The Family Health Issue

A Serious Subject worth Considering...

A NEIGHBOR AND I were discussing family communication issues. He's a retired guy and a writer. His comment, "It always surprises me how much is recalled when I clear my mind and apply pen to paper." In reality, he probably applies fingers to computer keyboard, but his message is clear. There's plenty to write about in emails and annual letters... the "How To" stuff. For example, secrets to managing the diminishing buying power of the monthly social security check or, how to find reasonably priced supplemental insurance, or how they're managing their health issues. Even emailing a link to an applicable informational site on the Internet is OK. I consider that communicating.

THINKING IN PRIVATE... The Present, Past and Future

Regarding health matters, I think younger family members have a right to know what to anticipate health-wise in their later years, particularly the inherited diseases and how these diseases are being managed by senior family members.

An issue of the AARP *Mature Outlook* magazine urged older family members to compile and circulate a list of major family physical and mental ailments so that younger family members are aware and can exercise precaution.

Over the years, through the "slip of the lip" method, I've discovered a number of ailments among family and in-laws: Addisons, COPD, Crohns, Diabetes, both Type I and II, serious Obesity, possible Parkinsons—the list goes on. BUT, It's anathema to even mention these illnesses on family visits or in phone conversations or emails. Typically, the subject is quietly listened to, then changed.

Thomas Jefferson, America's great statesman and communicator wrote that his worst mistake was not continuing daily exercise in his later years. He had lost his mobility, unable to mount and control a horse, or get into his carriage. What Jefferson missed most as he aged was taking frequent long walks with his dog in the woods around his Charlottesville, VA farm (Monticello), hunting small game with a hand gun.

Back in the late 1990s, several retirees were being interviewed on television. They discussed the benefits of their daily exercise regimen mentioning that consistent exercise was the best way to jump-start mind and body. So, armed with that excellent information, I included, along with that year's Christmas letter, a separate letter to a dozen or more of the older family members. I suggested the benefits of taking a walk several days a week; doing five minutes of daily stretching exercises; or, on alternating days, performing 10 to 20 minutes of either upper or lower body exercises. I even promised that the results would be positive. Metabolism would get a boost, blood flow and mental concentration would improve.

I rephrased the letter several times making sure it had a tactful and positive tone without sounding pushy. I awaited a response. Around the first of the year, an older family member called. I asked about the letter. "You and your exercises!" he

THINKING IN PRIVATE... The Present, Past and Future

blurted out. That was it. One reluctant respondent out of a dozen mailings. It's OK, I thought. I did my duty for family. At least I've gotten the word out.

How many retired do you know who do consistent daily exercise? There are walkers—according to my reading, about one in 10 takes 10-minute walks several times each week around their neighborhood or in the mall. However, there are few other consistent exercisers.

Shouldn't Thomas Jefferson's lament be a lesson learned and applied by both young and old? I think so.

Passing on our medical lessons learned brings to mind a story my father related to us boys years ago. Dad and mom, being good examples, had no hesitation discussing their aches and pains with their children. Dad had gone to our old family doctor complaining of knee and hand pain. The doctor thought a moment and said, "John, why don't you massage your bad knees with your bad hands, and get that circulation going?" It worked!

The next visit dad made to the doctor was to thank him for his good advice. Unfortunately, the doctor had to give dad

POSTS of ANDREW L. STEVANS

a cortisone shot in his bad shoulder. Bursitis had flared up from using his hands to massage his knees. As the saying goes, "Old age ain't for wimps." Dad lived fairly healthy into his mid-90's.

∞
RECALLED and OVERHEARD
∞

POSTS of ANDREW L. STEVANS

Critique:
Criticism and Cynicism

ABRAHAM LINCOLN OFFERED A SOLUTION to those disposed toward *criticism*, "He has a right to criticize, who has a heart to help." It wasn't until some years later that the cynical and frustrated Elbert Hubbard, the 19th century artist and writer offered this advice, "To escape criticism -- do nothing, say nothing, be nothing."

After reading comments by those who criticize critics, I have concluded that critics will never recover from the bad rap. Oliver Wendell Holmes, a known critic himself, wrote, "Nature, when she formed and created authors, contrived to make critics out of the chips that were left."

During my youth, Rosy Rosewell, a popular Pittsburgh Pirates baseball sports announcer well before and also during the time Bing Crosby owned the team, criticized his own audience to Crosby, "Critics are couch potatoes (spectators) with attitudes."

The final slam-dunk on criticism came from the Church itself, in the "critical" words of Archbishop C. Garbett, a popular English pastoral Bishop, "Any fool can criticize, and many of them do."

Anyone can be a critic, but not so with *cynics*, according to Bertrand Russell, a British philosopher and social critic, "*Cynicism* such as one finds very frequently among the most highly educated young men and women of the West, results from the combination of comfort and powerlessness."

It would be premature to conclude that cynics have received a kinder, gentler rap than have Mr. Holmes "chips". Cynics of the Western world may be a special breed, but it hasn't stopped their critics. Oscar Wilde wrote, "What is a cynic? He is a man who knows the price of everything and the value of nothing." H.L. Mencken, a 20th century journalist and a critic on American life, commented, "A cynic is a person who, when he smells flowers, looks around for a coffin."

The final comment – and one of the most cynical -- comes from Kenneth Clark, producer of the BBC series

POSTS of ANDREW L. STEVANS

Civilisation, "We can destroy ourselves by cynicism and disillusionment just as effectively as with bombs."

The conclusion appears to be that neither critics and their criticisms, nor cynics and their cynicisms are mutually exclusive. Sometimes critics are cynics, and, as demonstrated by Archbishop Garbett, will occasionally stoop to criticizing themselves. Cynics are sometimes critics, but – without my being critical, they are always cynics.

Tomorrow night I appear for the first time before a Boston audience -- 4000 critics. **Mark Twain**

Face to Face

Four Generations Interact

FOLLOWING THE GREAT AMERICAN tradition of labeling ourselves, a group of researchers have attempted to define our generational likes and dislikes. Surprisingly, *generational labeling* appears to have a positive effect. It works! We are now becoming aware of the positive and negative differences in the way our four current generations -- The Ikes, The Baby Boomers, the Generation Xers and (the new) Generation Ys -- approach life, career and leisure. We are also discovering what sociologist David Finkelhor terms "youth gone mild" a trend that appears to be turning the tide on impulsivity and indulgence.

POSTS of ANDREW L. STEVANS

On the positive side, the *Ike* Generation (aka: Ikes or the *Silent* Generation), those born during 1945 and earlier, are described as achieving their dreams through hard work. The *Baby Boomers,* born between 1946 and 1963, are individualists who welcome excitement and adventure. The *Gen(eration) Xers*, born between 1964 and 1978, are savvy entrepreneurs who appear to thrive on diversity. And, the *Generation Ys*, also referred to as *Millennials*, born after 1978, are the "wired generation", creative, and constantly generating change.

There is a downside to each generation. *Ikes* are resistant to change, and work to succeed to the point of becoming duty bound, whereas *Baby Boomers* consider success something they were born into and deserve, and are considered to be the self-absorbed generation. The Gen *Xers live* for change but, due to their escapist nature, are prone to job hop. And the *Millennials* are free spirits who live to celebrate life and view their job simply as an outlet for creative self-expression.

THINKING IN PRIVATE... The Present, Past and Future

Michele Harris writing for the Erickson Tribune, referred to a Pew Research survey that described how generations see themselves. She found that the *Ikes* are ahead of the other three generations in their patriotism, religious beliefs and environmental concerns. When the survey asked about America's greatness only 32% of millennials agreed that America is the greatest country. The number of those who agreed with the statement went up with their ages so that 72% of the Ikes agreed.

Crime on the decrease... On a more positive note are the comments of Sociologist David Finkelhor, the director of the Family Research Laboratory at the University of New Hampshire. Finkelhor says we may be seeing the rise of a more virtuous generation. He uses the 2002 – 2011 crime statistics from the Office of Juvenile Justice and Delinquency Prevention. Titling the report "Youth Gone Mild," he states that despite perceptions, today's young people are less prone to bad behavior than their elders. He also refers to the National Crime Victimization Survey and elaborates: "the number of sexual assaults against 12- to 17-year-olds has declined by more than half since the mid-1990s." He provides other examples: "violent victimization of teenagers at school has dropped 60 percent from 1992 to 2012. Peer victimization--harassment and bullying—have been abating in almost all of the surveys."

The bottom line… According to researchers, discovering our generational differences allows each generation to perform better in mixed-age work groups, and to communicate more effectively among multi-generation families. By having an understanding of how each generation thinks there is a more positive interaction among all generations.

"There is many a good tune played on an aging fiddle" **an old saying**

THINKING IN PRIVATE... The Present, Past and Future

Resolutions and Resolve

AT THE BEGINNING OF EACH NEW YEAR many of us feel a need to create a personal mandate for change. We list mundane resolutions and promise ourselves, with firm resolve, to begin a better way of living. Many of us facing this new year of a slowly building economy must implement a totally new way of living.

Tom Pfotzer, former president and publisher of the technical magazine "Techrocket," wrote an eye-opening article on Consumerism vs. Producerism. His article provides a new way of thinking about our New Year's resolutions.

Pfotzer defines *Consumerism* as the practice of consuming more than we produce—credit card debt, impulse buying, a keeping up with the Joneses mind set—and getting further and further in debt. Consumerists do not practice delayed gratification. They must have it "now." Consumerists will charge exotic foreign vacations, take out loans for gas-guzzling expensive new cars and own the latest electronic gadgetry including the largest screen TV. They buy their kids state-of-art computers to play video games, and spend excessive amounts of time maintaining lawns or building new decks on oversized homes.

Producerism, on the other hand, utilizes activities that tend to create independent living and true wealth. These individuals may well be the millionaires who live next door. Producerists consistently produce more than they consume. They create wealth as measured in dollars, social value, or in other constructive ways. Typically, they take U.S. based vacations, buy low maintenance, high economy used cars, and use their credit only in emergencies. Instead of gluing themselves to large screen TVs, and buying the kids computers for video games, they invest in interactive training courses, and help the kids build their own computers from components.

Back in the late 1700s, Ben Franklin wrote in his Poor Richard's Almanac: *"Waste not, want not."* In this New Year we

THINKING IN PRIVATE... The Present, Past and Future

can begin to create true wealth through planned investments of time, effort, and dollars. By doing so we can give the economy and ourselves a new way of living.

Americans must learn to live with their abundance without being forced to impoverish their spirit by making a virtue of wastefulness. **Vance Packard**: "The Waste Makers" 1960

POSTS of ANDREW L. STEVANS

Rude Awakening

SOME YEARS AGO, while preparing for an overseas assignment, it was explained that belching after meals was flattering to the Arab host; yet showing the bottoms of one's shoes was considered rude and offensive. It appears that what is considered *rude* in one culture may be completely acceptable in another. Of course, as in the following American examples, we may discover arguable situations within the same culture.

In its most basic form, rudeness is defined as "impolite, discourteous, or otherwise unacceptable behavior." According to Mark Caldwell, in his recent book: "A Short History of Rudeness," Martha Stewart's "rank commercialism and self promotion" is the art of civilized living that imitates upper-

THINKING IN PRIVATE... The Present, Past and Future

class manners, and is acceptable, given her agenda. Of course, this is just one opinion...

The American movies are an abundant source for two of the more serious forms of rudeness: One malevolent form is defined as *insolence or contemptuous behavior*. Liz Taylor won two Academy Awards for portraying an overbearing and scornful woman in "Who's Afraid of Virginia Wolf," and a brazen and condescending woman in "The Taming of The Shrew."

However, rudeness in its most degenerative form is defined as *savage or uncivilized behavior*. In the comedy spoof "Gremlins," the gremlin leader entered a laboratory and drank the Einstein Formula, immediately developing a polished British accent. Soon, he demanded an appearance on national TV, where he explained that the gremlin community only wished to be accepted as part of civilized society. He then drew his revolver and shot dead an irritating associate gremlin. His rational: "Of course, we are not quite civilized, yet."

Are there ever situations or conditions in civilized society that would allow rudeness? J. K. Rowling provides an answer of sorts in the movie "Harry Potter and the Half-Blood Prince"

    "Professor, why couldn't we just Apparate directly into your old colleague's house?" "Because it would be quite as rude as kicking down the front door," said Dumbledore. "Courtesy dictates that we offer fellow wizards the opportunity of denying entry."

Children are natural mimics who act like their parents despite every effort to teach them good manners. ~**Author Unknown**

THINKING IN PRIVATE... The Present, Past and Future

The Accelerator

(Near Future) Human Capability Analysis

A suggested approach...

THANK YOU FOR REQUESTING the Human Capability Analysis (HCA) ACCELERATOR. It's understood that you have already met with the medical professionals referred to you. Please take the enclosed package to a quiet, air-conditioned room that has a consistent temperature of 65 degrees. Minimum room size should be 10' X 12' and contain a full-size bed. Check the enclosed list carefully to make sure you have the computer and all other materials provided with the ACCELERATOR.

CAREFULLY FOLLOW ALL COMPUTER DIRECTIONS:
Key in "HCA ACCELERATOR" and follow the prompts. Place your hand on the screen when requested.

POSTS of ANDREW L. STEVANS

SECTION I: (1 hour) Mental Acuity and Stress (MAS). Check BODY-SUIT "A" for the correct size. Put on BODY-SUIT "A." All appropriate sensors are built into the suit. Follow monitor instructions for attaching BODY-SUIT "A" sensors to your body. The ACCELERATOR will measure your physiological responses during each question and answer. Enter MAS on the keyboard and follow the directions on the monitor.

SECTION II a: (1 hour) Physical Stress and Endurance (PSE). Enter your personal information on age, height, etc. Check BODY-SUIT "B" for the correct size. Put on BODY-SUIT "B." All appropriate sensors are built into the suit. Follow the monitor instructions for attaching BODY-SUIT "B" sensors to your body. Get on (mount) the ACCELERATOR Endurance cycle. Enter PSE on the keyboard and follow the directions on the monitor.

SECTION II b: (1 hour) Physical Coordination and Discipline (PCD). Check BODY-SUIT "C" for the correct size. Put on

THINKING IN PRIVATE... The Present, Past and Future

BODY-SUIT "C". The ACCELERATOR assumes that the referred physician has installed all appropriate subcutaneous sensors. Sensors will automatically interface with receptors in your suit as you put it on. Enter PCD on the keyboard and follow the instructions on the monitor.

SECTION II c: (1 hour) Sleep Patterns and Pathology (SPP). Place the fitted sheet on the bed. Embedded receptors are comfortably positioned around the perimeter of the sheet. Check BODY-SUIT "D" for the correct size. Put on BODY-SUIT "D" and the nylon cap provided. Enter SPP on the keyboard, and then lie on your back in the middle of the bed. You should have sufficient room to roll from side to side while sleeping. The ACCELERATOR presumes that the referred physician has instructed you and installed all subcutaneous sensors within the previous 6 – 8 weeks. Sensors will automatically interface with receptors in your suit and on the bed. The arrow on the cap must point to the subcutaneous sensor on your forehead. Place the sensor/oscillator eye pads on your eyes and fit the earphone plugs in your ears. Drink the

POSTS of ANDREW L. STEVANS

MM (Micro-Machines) soda provided. RELAX. You will awaken in 45 minutes.

SECTION III: Follow all instructions on your screen to complete The ACCELERATOR. Your detailed results will appear on the monitor along with your career, sport/s and armed forces/public service program. A life partner and the appropriate local coaches and instructors have already been electronically informed and will contact you shortly. Though hardly necessary, we wish you GOOD LUCK--and a GOOD LIFE!

Please repackage all materials in the Fed Ex box provided and return to ACCELERATOR Corporation.

Note: subcutaneous sensors and micro machines will dissolve or vacate the body within 14 days.

"All men should strive to learn before they die what they are running from, and to, and why." **James Thurber**, humorist

THINKING IN PRIVATE... The Present, Past and Future

The Happiness Gene

IN RECENT YEARS QUANTUN LEAPS have been made in the research to understand happiness. David Myers, professor of psychology at Hope College in Holland Michigan, is considered a leading researcher of happiness. He is a prolific author and a contributor to The National Opinion Research Center findings that periodically surveys happiness among the American population. Consistently the reports show that 3 in 10 Americans describe themselves as "very happy" – happier than Bill Gates, Oprah Winfry, and the Pope; 6 in 10 claim they are "pretty happy," and only 1 in 10 reports being "not too happy."

Happiness is affected by both *external* and *internal* factors. Researchers in the Psychology Department of the University of Chicago, explain that quality of work-life, an *external* factor, has a direct impact on our happiness. This is only true, however, if the work mindfully engages one's skills and challenges these skills without being overwhelming."

Researchers at both universities agree there is an *internal* or genetic predisposition to happiness. An example provided is the relationship between happiness and our cholesterol levels. Both are genetically influenced and yet both are, to some extent, under our control. It appears to be true that proper diet and exercise can have a strong, positive influence on our cholesterol levels, affecting as well our happiness. Happiness is a state of mind and body -- a state of being.

Who are the lucky happy people? They are the people who feel in control of their lives. They are naturally optimistic and extroverted, and tend to view situations realistically when bad things happen. They have a predisposition to empathize with and therefore be accepted by others. Of special note: Happy people are less self-focused and less self-preoccupied than unhappy people. Stewart Rosenthal, the publisher of Beacon Newspapers, has spent many years attempting to find the key to a happy life. His conclusion: "The key to a happy life is continuing to set and achieve worthy goals, within our ability, so that we always have something to look forward to."

Happiness researchers suggest that going through the proper motions can trigger the correct emotions. For example, feel optimistic, be outgoing and maintain a high level of self-worth. Happiness studies have shown that individuals feel better when they smile. So, some final advice: Put on a happy face.

Happiness lies in the joy of achievement and the thrill of creative effort. **Franklin D. Roosevelt.**

POSTS of ANDREW L. STEVANS

Internet Annoyances

A Glance Back

Each February our thoughts turn to Valentine's Day and to our love relationships. Yet, this year, the glitzy, glamorous kinds of business relationships came to mind. The blame may rest with the Internet doomsayers.

An earlier newspaper article (WP: redacted) headlined, "Should we mourn, cheer or fear the AOL-Time Warner marriage?" As it turned out it should be mourned. We listened to the doomsayers back then and rightly so.

Back then, Todd Gitlin, author of *Inside Primetime,* and professor of journalism, culture and sociology at New York University feared a submerging of serious news and debate into the all-engulfing business of entertainment. Gitlin

THINKING IN PRIVATE... The Present, Past and Future

predicted that news coverage would devolve into ever more streamlined and simple-minded snippets, and increase the media's love affair with celebrities and show business–a Hollywood *Love Net*. (Mr. Gitlin was ahead of his time—a true prophet!)

At the same time, Christopher Charron, director of media and entertainment group at Forrester Internet Research Company, cheered the exciting "media" merger. Americans would soon be able to listen to People Magazine's movie reviews through an Internet enabled car dashboard. The driver could cross-check a review against Roger Ebert's comments, gain access to AOL's Digital City, and make reservations via MovieFone (... all while talking on their cell phone, sipping coffee, inserting a CD, and lighting up–in the midst of Friday night rush hour).

Ellen Ullman, author of "Close to the Machine: Technophilia and Its Discontents" and a writer for *Harpers* and the *New York Times,* mourned that today's Internet is not the Internet promised, where everyone was supposed to be a publisher, and no one would control it. Ullman felt strongly that the promised Internet was dead, noting, as an example, that every "square pixel" of AOL's, Yahoo's and Microsoft's home pages had been sold off as ad sites.

But, why complain about the latest Internet irritations, when today's television has endless entertainment news, 20 channels of sports, and the cursed every few minute commercials? As "The Simpsons" creator Matt Groening lamented, "It is time to start contemplating just how annoying the 21st century is going to be."

Author's note: *Tim Berbers-Lee, inventor of the web protocols, decided to name the internet the "World Wide Web" when there were only three connections to it – a brave kind of hopefulness.*

THINKING IN PRIVATE... The Present, Past and Future

The Youth of Today

Our Future Leaders

FROM OPPOSITE SIDES of the social spectrum, plaintive cries are being heard about our young Americans. A former superintendent of the Naval Academy, Admiral John Ryan complains, "Our society has become course and unrestrained." He went on to comment that we must begin again to show more respect and dignity, more civility toward one another.

Ralph "Sonny" Barger agrees with the admiral. The retired national organizer and charismatic leader of Hell's Angels during the 1960's, defends the Hell's Angels explaining that they were bad but they did good too. Mentioning his eight-year-old daughter, he shows concern about her welfare, "Today, people are just so inhumane to each other. It's a terrible world to grow up in, especially now."

How do you respond to individuals with the extensive life experience of these two men? The question was posed to an insightful university professor, a world traveler and noted geologist. He sent the following response:

"The youth of today are irresponsible and lazy. They listen to no one and show disrespect toward everyone. They do not possess any of the qualities that we would want in our future leaders."

The professor attached an additional note: "The above quote was found among early Sumerian nail-writings, and is estimated to be over 4,000 years old."

America is a country where the youth are always ready to give to those who are older than themselves the full benefits of their inexperience.
Oscar Wilde

The Well-Offered Toast

TRACED BACK TO ANCIENT GREECE, the toast provides us a momentary pause and a memorable offering that elevates the moment.

Toasts have marked every conceivable occasion, the celebration of love, marriage and birth, work and play, parties and politics, holidays and New Years Day, retirement and old age -- even death.

Some toasts are brief...
"Here's to us all! God bless us every one! " -- Tiny Tim Toast, A Christmas Carol

POSTS of ANDREW L. STEVANS

> *"To long lives and short wars!"* -- Colonel Potter M*A*S*H
>
> *"Carpe Diem!* Seize the day!" -- Old Roman

Many toasts are offered in the New Year...
> *"In the New Year, may your hand always be stretched out in friendship, but never in want."* -- Gaelic
>
> *"Be at war with your vices, at peace with your neighbors, and let every New Year find you a better person".* -- Benjamin Franklin
>
> *"To the have-beens, the are-nows, and the may-bes!"* -- R.A. Campbell

Toasts are offered to love...
> *"To every lovely lady bright, I wish a gallant faithful knight; to every faithful lover, too, I wish a trusting lady true."* -- Sir Walter Scott
>
> *"Love doesn't make the world go 'round. Love is what makes the ride worthwhile."* James Thurber

And to love in old-age...

THINKING IN PRIVATE... The Present, Past and Future

"Do you love me or do you not? You told me once but I forgot." Anon

In a frenzied world there still remains a courtly gesture that has the rare magic to lift us and to mark the simplest of moments as special, the well-offered toast.

POSTS of ANDREW L. STEVANS

Y2K – The Way it was

Apprehension: December, 1999

IT APPEARS THERE'S NO WAY TO STOP IT-- the trend in Year 2000 (Y2K) "anxiety" buying. This anxiety is being fueled by the fear that some computer programs may incorrectly read the year 2000 as 1900 on January1, 2000.

One consumer, anticipating a Y2K power failure, purchased a home generator and hired an electrician to wire it into his home electric system. Another consumer, concerned with the failure of his gas furnace on New Years' day bought two top-of-the-line wood stoves. He installed one in his home, the other in his detached garage--just in case. Other consumers, preparing for a Y2K gasoline shortage, are buying and burying large gasoline tanks in their yards.

THINKING IN PRIVATE... The Present, Past and Future

One wonders how much Y2K impulse-buying is being driven by plain old fashioned business greed. Well meaning consumer advisory services may be inadvertently feeding the buying frenzy. One such service addressed a potential Y2K *software amnesia* in the car repair business. The article mentioned the possible failure of electronic files that track ordinary repairs, dealer service-shop warranties, as well as other non-factory services, and extended warranties. The report urges consumers to obtain printouts of their car-repair histories; to keep all paperwork for services as well as receipts for parts and accessories.

One answer to-anxious, fear-driven Y2K buyers is found in some sage advice offered to consumers a few thousand years ago: *Caveat emptor*, translation: "Buyer beware."

POSTS of ANDREW L. STEVANS

An Unforgettable Personality

AT NOTRE DAME, while attending Holy Cross Preparatory Seminary on campus, I learned how complex and diverse a personality can be. Father William McAuliffe, CSC, a larger than life, multi-talented Priest, assumed the role of Gregorian chant choir director at both Moreau (college) Seminary and Holy Cross Seminary.

Father McAuliffe made himself available at Holy Cross for one-hour each week to teach from the Liber Usualis, a few thousand page treasury of Catholic Gregorian chants, compiled over the years by the monks at the Abbey of Solesmes in France.

THINKING IN PRIVATE... The Present, Past and Future

Punctuality and Perfection... Father McAuliffe arrived at the Holy Cross chapel punctually at 7:00 pm, and expected each of us to be ready for a hands-on Gregorian music practice. In addition to his presumption that we already knew the several psalms that made up the basis for much of the Gregorian chant, Father assumed we were well versed in reading music.

"It's DO-ME-LA-DO, not DO-ME-SOL-DO. Let's do it again."

One evening Kaiser, a junior, arrived late for the one-hour session. He attempted to slip into an aisle at the back of the chapel.

"No, no, you come up here. If you're going to disturb us, you may as well do it right. Now, sit in the first row."

Father was a perfectionist when it came to Latin diction, allocution and accent. We each had a house copy of the Liber Usualis and were expected to use it.

An extreme incident happened when one of the Mullen brothers forgot to open his Liber Usualis and pay attention. This quickly brought down the Father McAuliffe wrath. In an instant a Liber Usualis was flying through the air toward the front pews. According to one account, Mullen ducked. There was a sudden quiet in the chapel.

A Step Forward... In post Vatican II years, Father McAuliffe embarked on a more demanding mission, emerging as an exceptional lecturer and demonstrating a great love of parish ministry.

It was several years after our class graduation. Father McAuliffe became involved in the fund-raising effort for the new Moreau Seminary building. He transformed the effort to focus on direct mail support. The highly successful direct-mail program soon included funds for the operational needs of both Moreau Seminary and Holy Cross Seminary. The effort was unique primarily due to Father McAuliffe's pastoral and individual outreach to each name on the mailing list.

Being a perfectionist in all he attempted, the results were first class. Patron participation reached many thousands of families.

Recalling the More Exciting, Earlier Years... Yet, during our seminary days--Father's less mellow years-- we vividly remember the "Canadian Goose incident." Some of us

THINKING IN PRIVATE... The Present, Past and Future

think it may have been a migrating Canadian goose using the on-campus St. Mary's Lake for a rest stop. As Father McAuliffe walked near the shore line, he was suddenly attacked. Father raised his brief case to protect himself, finally swinging it at the disturbed goose. The brief case handle broke and the brief case ended up in the lake, floating away from the shore line, sheets of music floating on the water.

Father McAuliffe, with his cassock tucked in his belt, and a fallen tree limb in his hand, waded into the water halfway up his pant legs to finally reach and retrieve some of the sheet music. The brief case sank to the bottom of the lake.

Notre Dame's Prefect of Discipline... During our senior year at Holy Cross, Father was assigned as disciplinarian (Prefect of Discipline) at Notre Dame. One evening, following a Notre Dame-Michigan football game (Michigan lost), Father found two Michigan football players wandering around campus, possibly looking for trouble. He confronted them and one took a swing at him--not a smart thing to do to anyone, and certainly not to a Priest on a Catholic University campus. Being a former athlete with good reflexes, Father McAuliffe ducked late and sustained bruises to his face. The incident was quickly brought under control. The "former" Michigan players returned to face charges.

To this day we discuss incidents involving Father William McAuliffe. We do believe this enigmatic man was a true man of God.

∞

HISTORY

∞

Perseverance

When Not Quitting Becomes a Habit

THERE'S A STORY of a frustrated college coach in the middle of a losing season, who screamed at his team: "Did the Wright Brothers ever give up?" The team yelled back, "No!" "Did Michael Jordan ever quit?" "No way!" "How about John Elway?" "No! No!" they shouted. "Did Billy Smith ever quit?" There was a long silence. Finally one player was bold enough to ask, "Coach, who's Billy Smith? We never heard of him." The coach snapped back, "Of course you never heard of him – he quit!"

The coach's remark brings to mind a comment by Louisa May Alcott, a poor but persevering and gifted writer of the nineteenth century. Alcott is the author of "Little Women," a book that appeared on best-seller lists one-hundred years

THINKING IN PRIVATE... The Present, Past and Future

after her death. She had a unique response when questioned about her decision to write full-time. A newspaper reporter asked how a writer could expect to etch out a decent living when great writers of the past like Shakespeare and Hawthorne (a close Alcott family friend) had made their incomes from real estate and surveying. She responded. "Early on, I resolved to take fate by the throat and shake a living out of her."

A forgotten poet spoke eloquently of perseverance: "Success is failure turned inside out – The silver tint in the clouds of doubt. And you never can tell how close you are; it may be near when it seems afar. So stick to the fight when you're hardest hit – It's when things seem worst that you mustn't quit."

Whatever you want to call it, willpower, dogged determination, plain old-fashioned grit, nothing in the world, not genius or education or talent or money, can take the place of perseverance.

"In the middle of difficulty lies opportunity." Albert Einstein.

POSTS of ANDREW L. STEVANS

THINKING IN PRIVATE... The Present, Past and Future

Northern Virginia History

Its Share of Unusual Happenings

THE ARCHIVES OF NORTHERN VIRGINIA contain folklore mixed with fact about Northern Virginia's Route 7 corridor. In the <u>early 1700's</u>, at the intersection of Old Court House and Gallows Road, a local courthouse and an adjoining prison were built.

In 1752 the courthouse was moved from Tyson's Corner. Virginia to Alexandria, Virginia. Gallows Road (originally called "The Long Road") was the route taken by prisoners being marched to the gallows from Tysons Court House to be hanged.

Early residents destroyed all remnants of the Tysons courthouse and prison--described as smelling like a pig sty-- supposedly to quell mysterious sounds heard in the area at odd times of the day and night.

POSTS of ANDREW L. STEVANS

In 1755, General Braddock's army followed the Old Indian Path (Route 7) which began near Williamsburg, VA and extended beyond the Allegheny Mountains. A short distance from Gallows Road, near Idylwood Road and the mansion of Col. Robert Lindsay (*The Mount*), Braddock changed his course west, toward Winchester, Virginia. It is near this point, *50 feet east of a spring, where the road runs north and south* that Braddock ordered buried two brass canon on end, filled with gold coin for payroll. Braddock and his men were later killed at the battle of Fort Duquesne, in Pittsburgh, Pennsylvania. The treasure has never been retrieved.

In the early 18th Century, before construction buried much of Carlin Springs, located just off Route 7, Indian children would offer to dive into the springs and retrieve Indian arrowheads and other trinkets for standers' by. Often the Indian children would remain under-water for long periods. The explanation of extensive caverns below the spring seemed to dispel concern. But the Indian children appeared only for certain people, and little is known where they went after their diving exhibitions.

THINKING IN PRIVATE... The Present, Past and Future

There is a plethora of tales that cloud the area. Until recent years "Beware the Night Air" was a common warning posted around the locale, providing a sense of foreboding to visitors to the area. Many strange (straynge) happenings over these past 250 years remain unexplained to this day.

POSTS of ANDREW L. STEVANS

National Treasures

Associations help America deliver on its promises

IN THE YEAR 1835, FRENCH STATESMAN Alexis de Tocqueville, author of the book "Democracy in America," remarked with some amazement on the large number and diversity of guilds, associations and clubs in America. He concluded that the new nation seemed to be succeeding so well at democracy because Americans of all ages, all stations of life, and all types of disposition were forming associations.

Chad Dickerson, the CEO of Etsy (*www.etsy.com/*), one of the newest, largest and fastest growing commerce sites online, states, "We're in an age where people have a hunger for belonging and meaning and connection."

The ASAE: American Society of Association Executives provides the rationale for these special interest groups. "Associations are formed for an enormous variety of purposes and provide a huge range of products and services for their members and, in many cases, for society at large."

"A sense of community coordination is at the heart of the association profession. People voluntarily join associations because they want to work together on a common cause or interest."

America's associations have deep roots in our history. The first American settlers formed "guilds," patterned after British traditions, to address common challenges and support each other's work and lifestyle.

This trend toward community coordination has shaped and advanced America since its birth and has historically set America apart from other nations. It is noted that since the birth of the Internet, associations or "non-governmental organizations" in many other countries are now growing in number.

While the complexity of associations and their role has evolved, today's associations still share the purpose of a coming together to produce positive results. The following comments represent differing views on associations in America...

"The instant formal government is abolished, society begins to act. A general association takes place, and common interest produces common security." **Thomas Paine,** journalist.

We're in an age where people have a hunger for belonging and meaning and connection. We can use commerce to bring communications together. **Chad Dickerson**, CEO of Etsy, a $500 million e-commerce website dedicated to the exclusive marketing of hand-made craft and vintage products.

THINKING IN PRIVATE... The Present, Past and Future

The Carillons of Central New York
A Christmas Memory

OFF OLD ROUTE 96 and the New York Thruway, located a short distance from the crystal- white sand beaches of Lake Ontario and the Port of Rochester, lie the small towns and villages of Central New York. Some were early settlements along the picturesque Erie Canal, and acted as gateways to the Finger Lakes recreational areas. Local families can often trace their lineage back to earliest America, and a large segment of the population's lives are deeply rooted in seasonal traditions and in Church and family. Our family lived there for several years in the early 1960s.

POSTS of ANDREW L. STEVANS

During the first year of our stay, the shopping centers – some boasting national chain stores – installed outdoor Christmas lights, loudspeakers, and Santa decorations well before Thanksgiving. The local officials would have no part of it and ordered all decorations removed. Because there was no immediate response to the request, churches began playing the death-knell, a single bell-toll each minute from dawn until dark. The shopping centers reluctantly extinguished their Christmas lights and lowered the music volume. But the death knell continued. Through the fall haze off Lake Ontario the tolling bells echoed down the Genesee Valley. Other towns and villages picked up its meaning and additional church bells began the plaintive knell, until finally the shopping centers relented. Loud speakers were muted and decorations completely removed.

The historic protest covered a few short days, yet the news of the happening spread far and wide. Sometime after Thanksgiving, church carillons began welcoming Christmas with seasonal songs. The local shopping centers quietly re-installed their Christmas lights and decorations, and added subdued holiday music. But the church bells are remembered as ringing in the true Christmas Spirit that year. And each

THINKING IN PRIVATE... The Present, Past and Future

year, throughout the region, you can hear them still, *"...and wild and sweet the words repeat, "Peace on Earth, Good Will to Men."*

I Heard the Bells on Christmas Day, **Henry Wadsworth Longfellow/ John Baptiste Calkin,** 1863

Two Moral Leaders

THE LATE ROBERT KENNEDY once commented, "Moral courage is a more rare commodity than bravery in battle or great intelligence." Yet, in retrospect, moral leaders seem to have appeared at needful times throughout history. They often faced similar problems and even shared common personal traits.

Two truly great moral leaders that shared a remarkable number of parallels in their lives were not only from totally different cultures but lived in different millennia:
--Both converted entire nations to their way of thinking.
--Both used dynamic, non-violent means to achieve their objectives in the face of seemingly insurmountable odds.

THINKING IN PRIVATE... The Present, Past and Future

--Both helped the people who often derided them.
--Both had traitors among their close acquaintances.
--Both were spiritualists with the highest integrity.
--Both were strong-willed and possessed great vitality.
--Both led austere lives, and refused material offerings.
--Both were convinced that a belief in truth was a belief in God.
--Both preached the innate goodness and potential within both women and men, and placed women on a higher plane.
--Both had philosophies for living that apply in any century.

The first leader was the fifth century's Patrick Calpurnius -- better known as St. Patrick -- the son of a wealthy British Celt official. St. Patrick was kidnapped at the age of 16 and enslaved in Ireland. After six years he managed to escape but later returned to Ireland to re-experience the basic goodness of the Irish people. St. Patrick taught the Christian and moral principles of peaceful coexistence, simplicity, self-sacrifice and truth. To spread his beliefs, he traveled extensively throughout Ireland, Brittany, Wales, and Scotland.

The second leader was the twentieth century's Mahatma Gandhi. At the age of 26, Gandhi campaigned against South African racial laws and the removal of voting rights from voters of color. Later, in his native India, he worked diligently to raise the standard for women. The popular and revered Gandhi undertook extreme fasts to promote India's Hindu-Muslim unification. Gilbert Murray wrote of Gandhi, "Persons in power should be very careful how they deal with a man who cares nothing for riches, nothing for sensual pleasures, and nothing for comfort and praise."

Moral courage is a uniquely human attribute. The brilliant nineteenth century Darwinian and highly respected biologist, Thomas Huxley, made the following observation, "Of moral purpose I see no trace in nature; this is an article of exclusively human manufacture – and very much to our credit."

THINKING IN PRIVATE... The Present, Past and Future

NOTES ON "TWO MORAL LEADERS"

Throughout history noted moral leaders have advocated similar philosophies that include humility, mutual respect, integrity, and peaceful resolution of differences.

- Epicetus: frugality, stoicism, equality
- St. Francis of Assisi: poverty, chastity, humility
- Martin Luther King: passive resistance, civil disobedience
- Nelson Mandela: equality, leadership by example
- Henry David Thoreau: voluntary poverty, [essay on] civil disobedience
- Leo Tolstoy: passive resistance, non-cooperation

POSTS of ANDREW L. STEVANS

Gang Warfare

How Three Communities
Resolved Aggressive Behavior

DURING A STUDY OF CHIMPANZEES, one particularly threatening chimp, Goe, was shunned by the chimp community. One of the older chimpanzees, Toe, who had protected a mother and daughter Chimpanzee from one of Goe's tirades, decided to leave the group. Toe took the two females with him and set up camp many miles away. After a few months, Goe and a few of his gang-members traveled to Toe's camp and killed Toe and the two females. Goe and his henchmen were ostracized from the community and were later discovered killed by other jungle animals. Quiet returned to the jungle habitat.

THINKING IN PRIVATE... The Present, Past and Future

In a National Geographic report, a group of young elephants was separated from their parents at a young age and transported by the forest service to a distant forest. As the young bulls and females matured, they formed into an unruly gang menacing and killing off the Rhinos and hippos, and any other living thing that got in their way. The forest service transported several fully mature bulls into the area. When the gang attempted to push around the older and larger bulls, they got pushed back and defeated. Calm returned to the forest community.

In Chicago's Cabrinni District, during a daylight shoot-out between two rival gangs, a figure dressed in tattered, handmade Mass vestments, the clothing of a Catholic Priest, quietly stepped into the streets between the warring factions. The predominantly Catholic gangs immediately called a cease-fire when "Brother Bill" Tomes, CSC, refused to leave the street. The word went out that anyone who hurt Brother Bill would be killed. Brother Bill was able to arrange meetings among gang leaders. Over time the inter-gang hatreds began to disappear. Many gang members returned to school or found work. Peace returned to the Cabrini District.

Peace exacts its own price, **Anon**

THINKING IN PRIVATE... The Present, Past and Future

Heroes and Hope

A Holiday Message

WE HEAR REFERENCES to the holiday season as the *Season of Hope*. Over 150 years ago, President Andrew Jackson defined hope clearly, "Hope is itself a species of happiness, and, conceivably, the chief happiness which this world affords."

Perhaps Andrew Jackson was thinking of a day when he was nine years old. A group of patriots, heroes all, pledged their personal fortunes, their sacred honor, their very lives to free 13 fledgling colonies from foreign rule and declaring a separate and free nation under God.

Today, hope is pervasive in many less obvious ways. There is remarkable hope and dignity among the many who lead meager lives of quiet desperation: the sick, the illiterate, the weak and elderly. There are single and widowed parents, often drawing from scant resources, raising children of character and compassion.

An inspirational TV commercial, starring Cliff Robertson, describes the country's blood donors as the quiet heroes. In truth, there are many quiet heroes whose personal sacrifices provide us with great hope and inspiration. They can be seen in emergency rooms and on rescue squads, in police departments, and among the peace keeping and volunteer forces from countries around the world.

Each year, during the holiday season, an ancient story is re-told that does not speak openly of heroes or courage and yet it inspires us. It tells of a young couple finding shelter in a stable on a cold winter's night. She is with child. A new heavenly star shines brightly in the East, awakening a sleeping world to the possibility of infinite hope.

"Hope is the thing with feathers
That perches in the soul –
And sings the tune without words
And never stops at all." **Emily Dickinson**

We are One through Humor

AN ANCIENT PROVERB SAYS, "The ointment of humor prevents friction and wins goodwill." A sense of humor is a gift far beyond worth. From an etymological view, the study of the origin and history of words, it appears that *Humor* is a word that may well describe a direct attribute of God, a gift bestowed on man.

The word *Humor* has significant God connotations. According to historians and researchers who study world religions, the word *Hu* (pronounced *Hugh*) is the earliest known name for God. Some one-syllable English words, derived from Old Germanic and Old Italic Indo-European languages may, in fact, relate to early man's image of a deity, for example, *Huge* [Old French: *great, vast*]; *Hue* [Old English: *shade, color, tint*]; *Hug* [Origin Unknown: to *embrace*]; *Hut* [Middle-High German and Old French: *shelter*].

Similar word meanings can be found in every ancient language spoken on earth: in the Old Indo-Iranian, Baltic, Greek, and Slavic Indo-European languages, as well as in Oriental, African, Algonquian, and all other North and South American Indian dialects.

It is interesting to note that, like *humor* [Latin: *mood, disposition*], many English words beginning with the syllable "*hu*" speak of creation or of civilized man, for example, *Humus* [Latin: *ground*]; *Humidity* [Latin: *water vapor*]; and *Human* [Latin: *Having the nature of man*], as well as words related to the word "Human", such as, *humane, humanitarian, humanism, humility* -- and even *hubris* and *humiliate*.

Returning in this "round-about" way to the subject of *humor*, we must all cherish our humorous side. Not only does humor appear to be the human reflection of a God-given attribute, humor also supports our human spirit by reinforcing our positive outlook. Another old proverb explains: "Though humor produces laughter, its true reward is a lightened heart."

Homo sapiens is the only one of God's creatures gifted with laughter. **Arun Gurjale**, former director of India U.S. (INDUS Corporation)

POSTS of ANDREW L. STEVANS

Love and Caring

Each year in mid-february our attention focuses on the Valentine's Day message of romantic *love*. But another form of deeply rooted love may take high precedence over its romantic counterpart.

Unlike sexual love, there are many relationships that define caring love, the love that "sacrifices oneself for another"--the love between parent and child, among siblings, among relatives, among friends, and often among total strangers. A caring love includes commitment to duty and to country, to truth and to justice – and even to animal rights. .

On TV recently, a breath-taking rush-hour event showed a squirrel hit by a car at a busy intersection and a

THINKING IN PRIVATE... The Present, Past and Future

second squirrel racing back into high-speed traffic, attempting to pull its injured companion to safety. An episode on National Geographic fascinated the nation when a herd of elephants worked for many hours, in a series of death-defying acts, to free one of their members from a deep, mud pit. It's unfortunate that this love was described as *loyalty*. When man is involved, it's described as compassionate or caring love.

The real St. Valentine message was one of caring love. It can be called sensitivity, empathy, concern, kindness -- or even loyalty. But, whatever the word, it is the most meaningful love because caring love is the love that makes possible our survival.

POSTS of ANDREW L. STEVANS

Courage of Conviction

IT IS NO MISTAKE THAT COURAGE appears in the word discouragement. In our high-tech, topsy-turvy world, it can take great courage to be true to our convictions. Teddy Roosevelt spoke clearly of those with courage and conviction (redacted):

"…The prize is not to the critic, those cold and timid souls who know neither victory nor defeat; it is to that individual in the midst of the turmoil, often unheralded, and frequently disapproved by friend and foe alike, who risks all to follow his strongest conviction to its rightful conclusion…"

Thomas Edison was known for his stubborn courage and strong conviction. He spent years investing every penny and all of his time creating a first-rate laboratory. Late one night in a devastating fire he lost everything. Arriving on the fiery scene he appeared undiscouraged. "What a wonderful gift in disguise! We can rebuild everything with new materials and replace our outdated equipment." This human dynamo lifted everyone's spirit by sheer force of will. Edison then crawled onto a nearby table and fell immediately into a deep sleep.

We must carefully plan each step when attempting new ways of doing things, or when simply trying to do the right thing. We must anticipate criticism and disapproval, and we must view our fear and apprehension as a stimulant, never as a discouragement.

"*One man with courage makes a majority.*" **Andrew Jackson**

POSTS of ANDREW L. STEVANS

Nature vs. Nurture

Life Requires Both

A VOTE FOR NATURE... How much of our natural ability is obtained through our genetic makeup, our heredity? The comment: "She's a natural athlete," is considered a vote for nature.

A recent study conducted by Princeton University seems to agree with other scientific conclusions on performance. If an average athlete and an above average athlete practice for the same amount of time, the above average athlete will still continue to outperform the average athlete.

The same appears to be true if you wish to become an expert artist or an expert musician. While plenty of practice is

THINKING IN PRIVATE... The Present, Past and Future

essential to become very good at anything, it turns out that nature - not nurture - plays a bigger role than was originally thought.

Put another way, if you don't have the *natural* ability to become, say, a great artist, you may want to consider some other line of work.

A VOTE FOR NURTURE?... Nurture is described as individual traits learned through our social environment. We hear words such as behavior, intelligence, will power, temperament, and other areas such as faith and hope. These attributes are considered by some social scientists to be traits primarily acquired through nurturing, beginning at an early age. For example, an introverted or shy individual may struggle to show empathy or compassion.

For years a debate has raged about very young children abandoned in the wild, only to emerge years later as mumbling mutes, unable to learn to speak a human language. Does nurturing account for our ability to speak?

NATURE OR NURTURE... Some years ago there was a research study performed on the same species of monkeys living on two islands. We'll call the islands "Island-A" and "Island-B." There appeared to be no exchanges between these two colonies of monkeys. There was no way for the monkeys to actually travel from one island to the other due to the great distance between the islands and also the fact that the local aquatic life enjoyed eating monkeys.

The monkeys on Island-A were discovered using a new wood prying tool to open coconuts after the coconut was cracked with a stone. In later years it was discovered that the monkeys on Island-B were using a similar wood prying method to open their cracked coconuts.

Is this really a vote for Nurture? Since they were the same species of monkey, wouldn't they learn at about the same pace? Wouldn't they evolve at the same rate as their sister species on Island-A? It may be a considerable leap to attribute this to Nurture

ONE CONCLUSION… Researchers in the psychology department at Vanderbilt University recently stated: "The view that anyone can learn to do essentially anything is not scientifically defensible.

"Live a godly life and nurture kindness, compassion, justice, and humility." **Jim George**, American award winning author.

THINKING IN PRIVATE... The Present, Past and Future

Noblesse Oblige

Conducting ourselves nobly.

PARENTS GIVE US LIFE AND BREATH and help instill within us our moral compass. Life experience and religious beliefs continue to build our characters and inspire us to seek truth. Educators identify and implement required curriculum to meet the needs of the communit.y. Business leaders provide the earning opportunities that allow us to succeed.

What more can there be to a life? A French phrase answers the question wisely: *Noblesse oblige.* Literally, Noblesse Oblige means "nobility obliges." It is the concept that nobility status extends beyond mere entitlement. Noblesse

Oblige requires that individual blessed with status and means fulfill social responsibilities to others who are less fortunate.

Bill Gates, founder of Microsoft, referred to this obligation explaining that in every person there is a driving need to be successful and an obligation to give back to others. "Our family believes that if life happens to bless you, you should use those gifts as well and as wisely as you can."

Bill Gates Senior, Bill Gates father, said it another way: "I believe our society works better when people think less about "me and mine" and more about "us and ours."

ALL THE WRONG REASONS: Too many of us pursue helter-skelter the status of "rich" or "millionaire" or "early"retirement" never thinking about those less fortunate who are in dire need of our assistance.

So, what can we do? How can we contribute? The following list of ideas is offered through *Shepherd's Centers,* a prominent support charity. Shepherd's Centers are located in large and small cities across the nation.

THINKING IN PRIVATE... The Present, Past and Future

Through our help Shepherd Centers offer support to the elderly, to the disabled, and to those confined in our communities. Some areas of assistance are...
-- Transportation to medical visits.
--Assistance with down-sizing/de-cluttering.
--Planning assistance.
--Friendly caller/visitor.
--Caregivers' support
--Handy man services offering minor repairs
--Health advocacy

Following is a quote from the "Shepherd's Centers of America" home page http://www.shepherdcenters.org/...

"With the shifting demographics and economic changes affecting health and social services these days, many more of our older Americans are falling between the cracks and living in isolation."

"*Loneliness, fear and the feeling of being unwanted is the worst poverty,*" **Mother Teresa.**

POSTS of ANDREW L. STEVANS

Ennobling Obsession

Ennobled Spirit or Irrational Instinct?

THE PHILOSOPHY PROFESSOR was attempting to demonstrate to the class the idea of rational human thought and irrational or instinctive animal thought. Earlier, the students had finished their assignments in reading and had viewed two movies in preparation for the class. The professor asked "What theme does the book *Dr. Hudson's Secret Journal*, by Lloyd C. Douglas and the movies *Magnificent Obsession* and *My Fair Lady* have in common?"

There were many answers, often with extensive explanations that went on for most of the class session. The professor finally provided his answer, "*Ennobled spirits;* helping a fellow human being is ennobling." The professor

THINKING IN PRIVATE... The Present, Past and Future

paused for effect. "In *Dr Hudson's Secret Journal,* Doctor Hudson benefits far more than his patients when he secretly financially assists patients who are facing desperate financial situations in their lives. In *Magnificent Obsession,* a recently blinded woman is helped by a rich playboy turned MD who secretly assists her to regain her sight, thereby opening his own eyes to his true inner motives. And, in *My Fair Lady,* a linguistics professor unceremoniously drags a young woman from the streets on a bet to make her into a debutante, only to realize that her integrity is her real beauty."

In each case claimed the professor, the benefactor grew spiritually in a way that no irrational animal possibly could. The professor again described and emphasized the term "irrational" as not possessing rational thought, instinct, not possessing the human soul.

Following the rigorous session, a small group of students remained in the class room. This group had watched animal behavior on TV nature shows. In their personal lives, they had seen their own pets demonstrate anxiety, fright, jealousy, sadness, even mourning the death of a mate or companion. Could the professor's "irrational thought" argument be true?

The students stated their case to the professor: "Put aside the theory of human rational thought vs. irrational animal instinct. Isn't the cheetah suddenly and forever ennobled in her attempts to hide and quiet her cubs from the foraging lions and hyenas? How about the cheetah's attempts to distract these hunters by showing herself as a target, far from her cubs' lair? Doesn't she mourn the loss when she discovers that her cubs are dead?"

The professor smirked, mumbled something about a lot of hogwash, and left the classroom.

THINKING IN PRIVATE... The Present, Past and Future

∞
UNSOLICITED COMMENTARY
∞

POSTS of ANDREW L. STEVANS

UNSOLICITED COMMENTARY titles span much of what appears to be current thought. Surprisingly, It's a collection recorded over 20 year period. Yet, much of the subject matter appears to be applicable to our lives even today.

"*Giving Back*" discusses the youth maturity issue. "*Reality Checks,*" delves into Social Security concerns--little has changed in this regard since the essay's publication in 2000. In February 2002, the post "*Love Thy Neighbor, or Else,*" provides a world view of U.S. efforts abroad. Both essays appeared in the U.S. India corporate newsletter, mentioned in the Introduction. .

"*Decision-making under Stress*" was part of a cassette learning course and workbook published in 1988. The course has been presented over the years within the NVCC (Northern Virginia Community Colleges) adult learning centers and also through ASAE: American Society of Association Executives.

"*Fear Tactics and the ISMs*" as well as "*High Performance Cultures*" and "*Pretense"* were more recent posts, having been written in 2006.

THINKING IN PRIVATE... The Present, Past and Future

"*The Computer Elite*" began as a phone discussion back in the 1980's with Brit Hume. At the time, Hume, who later became the ABC Chief White House Correspondent, was busy writing his computer column for the Washington Post.

Unsolicited Commentary is a collection of personal thoughts gathered and recorded over time. They may not meet the strict standards of journalism. I'm not a journalist. However, I'm in good company. Jon Stewart, of "The Daily Show," a source of news for millions also doesn't appear to meet that strict standard. My hope for the following posts is that the subject matter raises interest and adds somewhat to our reservoir of understanding.

POSTS of ANDREW L. STEVANS

Giving Back
Is this a Maturity Issue?
October 19, 2013

IN AN EARLY SEPTEMBER Outlook section of the Washington Post, I read Anne-Marie Slaughter's: "America should care more about caring." The article emphasized America's ability to re-invent itself. It was well written and started me thinking about the "Next American Nation" as described by Slaughter. Perhaps, first on the list should be the search for better ways to allow all of our youth to mature and to act as responsible, empathetic individuals?

PART OF THE PROBLEM... Recently, I sat near a father and son out to breakfast. During the meal, both were on their smart phones. There was little discussion--actually, no discussion--between them. Their faces were expressionless.

THINKING IN PRIVATE... The Present, Past and Future

Breakfast was eaten in between quick, almost feverish texting or searching maneuvers being performed on their respective smart phones. Multiply this scenario by millions of individuals in their cars, on street corners, walking into traffic, etc., and you begin to see the picture.

It bothered me and made me think of family discussions of lore as we sat around the table relating the anecdotes of the day, looking at the faces and into the eyes of our listeners—actual human contact—asking questions, making comments, laughter, giving a reassuring touch or embrace.

Thanks to the invisible world of smart-phones, the maturing population doesn't appear to be maturing, that is, using actual voice and eye-to-eye communications, thinking of the other guy, a spirit of cooperation, developing a strong work ethic, to mention a few of these vast areas of concern. The smart-phone is dumbing America where it counts most, namely, the showing of simple courtesy to others and demonstrating our genuine concern.

POSTS of ANDREW L. STEVANS

ONE SOLUTION... The SSL program: Student Service Learning is a start. SSL requires middle and high school students volunteer a set number of community service hours in order to graduate. The program is available in 35 states and the requirements vary state to state. The follow-on program would set a national standard for SSL with mandatory post high school enrollment in all states.

Currently, when a young man reaches 18 years of age, he's required to sign up for *Selective Service*. This system could be used to require all post high-school age students, both young men and young women, to sign-up for and *select* a public service from among many alternatives as a way of giving back. The required service would last six months or longer, and allow our youth to give back to a nation that has given them so much. Through a required indoctrination class taught in high school, mandatory public service (not necessarily military, and possibly served locally) would open their eyes to what America is all about.

I believe our up and coming generations would emerge from the experience caring more for and about each other.

THINKING IN PRIVATE... The Present, Past and Future

And, in addition to becoming more socially aware and stronger team players, they may become less prone to self indulgence. They would become mature young adults better prepared to launch into their life's journeys.

"The best things in life aren't things" **Art Buchwald**

POSTS of ANDREW L. STEVANS

Belief: All in the Eye of the Beholder

THE *ATHEIST* SAYS WE ARE BORN, we live and we die. The *theologian* adds a reason for being, stating that we are born in the image and likeness of God, we live a life searching for truth, and when we die, the faithful emerge victorious in heaven. The *Humanist*, caught between the atheist and the theologian, believes the ancient Greeks had it right. We are born through no fault of our own; we live a life focused on logic not faith. During our life's journey we respect all others, aspiring to a life of personal and ethical fulfillment thus contributing to the greater good of humanity. But, after expending all this effort, the humanist believes that when we die we simply return to the dust from which we came.

THINKING IN PRIVATE... The Present, Past and Future

Isaac Asimov, the prolific and gifted writer, a professor of biochemistry, and a staunch humanist, was at one time the elected leader of the Humanist movement. Asimov was asked the question: "So, if you do something sinful or wrong the humanist has no escape hatch?"

"That's right. If I do something wrong, I have to face myself and I may not be able to figure out a way of forgiving myself. In my way of life, there may be repentance but it doesn't make up for the sin. If you are ethical only because you believe in God, you are buying your ticket to heaven or trying to tear up your ticket to hell. I think that people who say virtue is its own reward or honesty is the best policy have the right idea."

Asimov died in 1992 leaving behind a treasure trove of published textbooks, the Asimov Bible, popular science articles and books, science fiction and literary criticism. Kurt Vonnegut, another noted American writer and outspoken humanist, was asked to speak at Asimov's funeral. Many of the attendees were from the humanist movement. Vonnegut began, "We can all be happy now that Isaac is in heaven." It took a moment, but the comment, typical of Vonnegut, brought waves of laughter.

Vonnegut became the outspoken leader of the humanist movement following Asimov's death. Vonnegut also denied the existence of God, an afterlife and Christian doctrines about sin and salvation. Vonnegut served as honorary president of the American Humanist Association (AHA), until his own death in 2007. In a letter to AHA members, Vonnegut wrote, "I am a humanist, which means, in part, that I have tried to behave decently without expectations of rewards or punishments after I am dead."

"Live among men as if God beheld you; speak to God as if men were listening." **Seneca**, first century: Roman Statesman, philosopher

THINKING IN PRIVATE... The Present, Past and Future

Fear Tactics--the ISMs

Fear and fanaticism

ON THE RIGHT SIDE OF THE HUMAN BRAIN is a small fingerprint-size area that, according to brain research scientists, contain the traits that make us human; traits such as compassion, love, guilt, and our other emotions. Also within this tiny area resides the neural tissue that allows radicalization and can drive individuals to acts of brutal aggression (See: *Medical Murder*).

Today, the world is focused on the Middle-East form of fanaticism and fear mongering, namely, Islam extremists.

WAHABISM: Muslim Extremists weren't born that way. Ninety-nine point nine percent of Muslims, of which there are over one billion believers around the world, are law abiding citizens. The *Wahabi* movement began in Saudi Arabia during the early part of the 20th century. Wahabism is a rigid and hatred strewn teaching of Islam that is now blamed for much of the extremism that goes on around the world-- under the guise of "enforcing" the Muslim faith. The objective of these extremists is to control everyone and everything through fear and their version of Sharia Law.

Back in September 2002, the year after the Twin Towers fell, it was reported that Mullah Mohammed Akrey made a strong statement against Wahabism. Akrey, the most senior of five clerics at the Islamic Scholars Union meeting, held in Iraqi Kurdistan said, "Islam and Judaism and Christianity have flourished together for more than 1400 years. These Wahabis are not Muslims and do not represent Islam."

While the West has little to feel threatened by traditional Islam, the events of 9-11 demonstrate that we have much to fear from Wahabism.

CHRISTIAN EXTREMISTS: Back when *Wahabism* began, another faction hell-bent on acquiring control by

THINKING IN PRIVATE... The Present, Past and Future

instilling fear was called the *Mafioso,* an extremist movement that originated in Sicily and controlled much of the commerce in Chicago and New York, and in many of the larger towns and cities across the U.S., as well as in Italy. Their objective was to control legal and illegal commerce by any means possible, primarily through fear tactics.

President George W. Bush, when questioned about the similarity between the Mafia movement and the Wahabi fanatics, indirectly appeared to defend the Mafia when he made the statement that their objective was money, not religious fanaticism. It's interesting that the means to the end, control of others through fear, was not elaborated on by this president.

Horrific acts by extremists have happened throughout human history. Often there's an agenda, typically greed and politics. Examples abound. During the first through third centuries, the Roman authorities routinely searched out and persecuted or murdered Christians and Jews. In the 13th century, hundreds of thousands of individuals were investigated, some killed, during the 170 years of the

POSTS of ANDREW L. STEVANS

Medieval Inquisition. During the 16th and 17th centuries, the Spanish Inquisition conservatively caused the deaths of 5,000 individuals. Other estimates are much higher. America experienced its own purges when, during the early 17th century, in and around Salem Massachusetts, dozens of women, supposed witches, were put to death by drowning, burning or hanging. In 1968, in what became known as the My-Lai massacre, our American military, tired of not being able to recognize the Viet Kong enemy, killed an entire village of 500 Vietnamese men, women and children.

COMMUNISM and SOCIALISM... Anne Applebaum, wrote an article for the Washington Post, "Is it 1939 again in Europe?"Applebaum commented that Russian analyst Andrei Piontkovsky published a recent article arguing along the lines that Russian President Vladimir Putin really is weighing the possibility of limited nuclear strikes against one of the Baltic capitals or Poland. "Indeed, in military exercises in 2009 and 2013, the Russian army openly "practiced" a nuclear strike on Warsaw. Putin appears to have one objective; to prove that

THINKING IN PRIVATE... The Present, Past and Future

NATO is a hollow, meaningless entity that won't dare strike back for fear of a greater catastrophe."

North Korea under the Kim Il-Sung, Cuba under the Castros, China under Mao Zedong and the Soviet Union under Stalin, all of these individual's have a common thread. Eliminate anyone and everyone who was a threat to their power by spying on their own people. There was no safe haven. Torture, murder, slave labor, imprisonment or the deaths of all relatives were a part of the fear tactics of these Communist regimes. Stalin alone murdered 10s of millions of his people. Totalitarianism was equal to or a close second to Communism's fear tactics as demonstrated by the Sadam Hussein regime in Iraq, the governments of Sudan, Libya, and Egypt—the list goes on.

CAPITALISM (the greed factor)...When we speak of fear tactics we must include the historic trends in American Capitalism--America's own unique form of domestic terrorism. Capitalism is a kinder, gentler approach to fear mongering, where the "community" is defined as the corporation. In its simplest form, corporate lobbyists control our government representatives. The lobbyists are dedicated to increasing corporate profits and having the corporations pay little or no taxes. There is little concern for the general population and, among the corporate elite, little concern for their employees.

Examples are the halting nature of the congress to increase the U.S. minimum wage to a livable wage; or to provide equal pay for women doing the same job as their male counterparts. Capitalism instills a sense of insecurity and fear among America's working class. The indigent, including an increasing number of the working class, as well as those on fixed incomes, single-parent families, the sick and elderly are not a consideration among capitalism's elite rank and file—unless there is a political rationale to do so.

There is a plan among the super wealthy in America. The 21st century Political/Industrial Capitalist movement is currently concentrated on controlling the banks, the cost of commodities, gasoline, electric and natural gas, prescription drugs, medical and other areas of the economy that directly impact all of us. We Americans really have to concentrate

THINKING IN PRIVATE... The Present, Past and Future

more on healing our own cancers, becoming better educated and more aware of our own government's capitalist fear tactics, before taking on the rest of the world's many forms of fear and terror mongering.

There is a naïve trust in the goodness of those wielding economic power.
Pope Francis

We can still safely say that the top 10% of the world's adults control about 85% of global household. That compares with a figure of 69.8% for the top 10% for the United States. The power of the corporate community and the upper class has been increasing in recent decades.
G. William Domhoff, research professor in psychology and sociology at the University of California, Santa Cruz.

POSTS of ANDREW L. STEVANS

Love Thy Neighbor, or Else
A Message to the Free World

IF, IN THE LATE 1980s, AN ECOLOGIST had been asked to name countries with the most fragile environments and the most urgent public health needs, the answer would have included Afghanistan, Burundi, Haiti, Iraq, Nepal, Rwanda, Somalia, Yugoslavia and Zimbabwe. The close match between that list and the list of the world's political hot spots today, many of which are war and disease ridden, is no accident.

The U.S. and its allies have created a major problem with our broken promises. Imagine the anguish and feeling of betrayal if a well established foreign organization took away your livelihood, destroyed your town, killed some of your

THINKING IN PRIVATE... The Present, Past and Future

friends and neighbors and then disappeared. Yet, this is what the free world has imposed on war-ravaged countries that have "cooperated" with the U.S. and its world partners in past years.

There is an answer. According to UCLA's Jared Diamond, Professor of Public Health and Physiology and author of the Pulitzer Prize winning book: *"Guns, Germs, and Steel: The Fate of Human Societies"* provides a straight forward solution; one that is economical when compared to the expense of war. The solution has been proven in a dozen endangered countries around the world.

According to Diamond, we must initially guarantee an ongoing and equitable distribution of food to the masses. We must then provide public health, basic education including family planning, and restore control over the natural environment: providing sources of clean water, teaching crop rotation, and halting soil erosion. This approach has produced immense benefits to the recipient country and has earned us unending good will.

POSTS of ANDREW L. STEVANS

Not long after World War II Winston Churchill wrote: "How the great democracies triumphed and so were able to resume the follies which had so nearly cost them their lives."

We must be ever more vigilant today to avoid falling into the victors' follies.

THINKING IN PRIVATE... The Present, Past and Future

Reality Check

The Demise of Our Social Security Program

THE SOCIAL SECURITY PROGRAMS in the U.S. as well as similar programs across Europe and in Japan are at such high-risk levels of insolvency that it is causing international waves of concern. Yet, the Congress and administration (1997) spent hundreds of billions of Social Security entitlements to balance the Federal budget. The perceived reality and the general feeling among politicians are that the U.S. Social Security program is safe until 2033. The reality is that Social Security, personal savings habits and Federal health care are all on extremely shaky ground.

Former President Jimmy Carter commented in his 1998 book, "The Virtues of Aging," that about half of the Federal budget goes to pay for programs for the elderly. He warned that if basic changes are not made in entitlement programs by 2013, the entire Federal budget will soon go to pay for the elderly and for interest on the Federal debt.

Recent recommendations... In November 2014, the Center for Retirement Research with the support of the Washington Post presented an array of 12 courses of action to fix Social Security. Of the 3,600 responses, two recommended courses of action were the most popular.

The most popular solution, chosen in 71% of reader responses, was to make highest earners pay more Social Security taxes. Under the current system, American workers do not have to pay Social Security tax on earnings beyond $117,000. That covers about 82.5@ of all U.S. earnings. (It's interesting to note that 92% of earnings were covered at the beginning of the program in 1937.) By raising the level to cover 90% of earnings over a 10-year period, the cap would increase to $250,000 according to the 2014 Trustees Report.

The second most popular choice by a 45% vote was to raise the retirement age. Maybe this solution recalled a similar

THINKING IN PRIVATE... The Present, Past and Future

measure taken in 1983, the last time there was federal action to address Social Security's financial problems.

Personal savings a concern... With all the evidence to support Carter's belief, the Baby Boom generation – those born between 1946 and 1963—have saved less than 5 percent of earnings, less than a quarter of their Japanese counterparts. This is true among most of America's young adults even though only 28% think that they can depend on a Social Security check when they retire.

An aside: Carter and federal Health care costs... Reflecting private sector increases, the federal government's spending on health care has also skyrocketed. In 1965 the government spent $100 per person for health care, or about one-percent of the Gross Domestic Product (GDP). In 1975 spending had risen to $1,000, or two-percent of GDP; in 1981, the final year of the Carter administration, to $2,500 or three- and one-half-percent of GDP; and in 1995, Carter's last recorded tally in his book "Virtues of Aging," to $7,000, or 5.3-percent of GDP. Currently, government spending on health care is at 7.3-percent of GDP. Putting aside the politics of the day, the hope is that the Affordable Care Act will gradually reduce federal spending on health care.

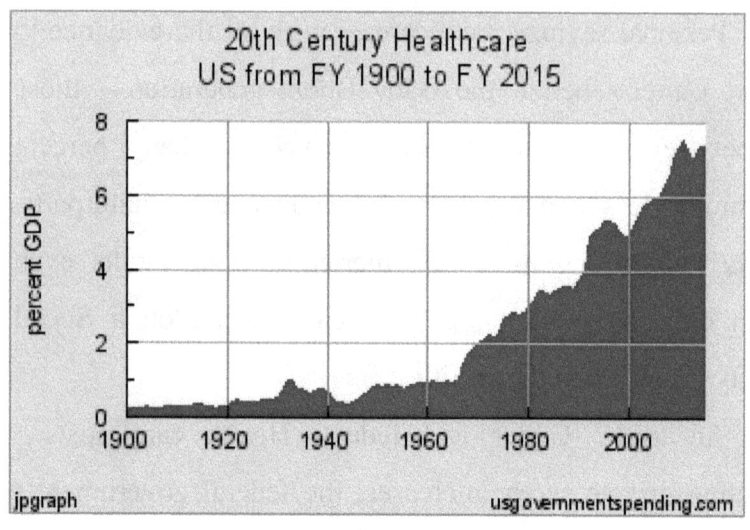

As a final note on Social Security, in 1935 when the American Social Security system was first established, the tax contributions of 40 wage earners supported each retiree. By 1990 there were only 3.3 workers for each recipient, and by 2010 only 2 people are paying for the retirement and medical expenses of one senior citizen. Without careful study and modification soon, the official projections are that the total

THINKING IN PRIVATE... The Present, Past and Future

Federal cost of Social Security will rise to 50-percent of the taxable payrolls of American workers.

Let's hope that our euphoria from the recent high income-high spending era has been replaced with the reality of our upcoming retirement income predicament.

POSTS of ANDREW L. STEVANS

Military Pay

FOR SOME TIME FOLLOWING the Reagan years, the military establishment insisted on funding the Star Wars Initiative. More recently super-modern missiles, tanks and advanced jet-plane programs have taken precedence over improving our military facilities and providing decent cost-of-living wage increases for our career enlisted personnel.

The 2014 enlisted-personnel wages compared to officer wages serve as an example. The following tables reflect the active 2014 Military Pay Scale (1.0% raise) for all United States military active personnel. Enlisted personnel are "E" grades ranging from E-1 to E-8. Officers are "O" grades ranging from O-1 to O-8. Income is shown as Monthly Pay without any benefits/bonuses.

THINKING IN PRIVATE… The Present, Past and Future

2014 Military Pay Scale

ENLISTED WITH 10 YEARS SERVICE: Monthly Pay

E-1	E-2	E-3	E-4	E-5	E-6	E-7	E-8
1531.50	1716.90	2034.90	2427.30	3076.20	3331.50	3709.80	4134.30

OFFICER WITH 10 YEARS SERVICE: Monthly Pay

O-1	O-2	O-3	O-4	O-5	O-6	O-7	O-8
4195.20	5028.60	5862.60	6593.10	6949.50	7547.70	9767.60	11373.90

www.militaryfactory.com/military_pay_scale

Promotions among the career enlisted have historically followed a procedure where those promoted with the most seniority in rank put on the patch (rank) and receive the pay increase first. Depending on time-in-grade, under this system, a promoted enlisted could wait up to a year to receive the rank and the corresponding pay increase.

How many companies in industry would survive if an employee was given a promotion and pay raise that didn't become effective for a year?

POSTS of ANDREW L. STEVANS

Congressional Retirement
Addressing a Recent Misinformation Campaign

CURRENTLY A SENATOR OR CONGRESSMAN earns $170,000 annually. Party Leaders receive $193,400 annually. According to the Congressional Research Service, since 2009 Congressional salaries have been frozen and many allowances have been frozen or reduced in recent years.

So much inaccurate information has been bandied about in blogs, discussions and emails regarding congressional pensions and benefits that several research organizations: Politifact.com, FactCheck.org and Snopes.com, with the cooperation of the non-partisan Congressional Research Service decided to get the actual facts. The following information summarizes their findings.

THINKING IN PRIVATE... The Present, Past and Future

RETIREMENT PENSIONS... A report on "Retirement Benefits for Members of Congress," prepared in November 2013 by the nonpartisan Congressional Research Service, outlines how pension benefits are calculated. The key provision: no member of Congress is eligible for any pension unless he or she has served in Congress for at least five years. (Senators serve six-year terms; House members must seek reelection every two years.)

PENSION RULE: *To collect a pension, a congressman or senator must be age 62, or be at least age 50 with 20 years of service, or be any age with 25 years of service.*

Under the most recent pension program, adopted in 1984, the size of a pension is based on the highest three years of a member's salary, the number of years of service and a multiplier, which is 1.7 percent for the first 20 years of service and 1.0 percent for subsequent years.
EXAMPLES OF PENSION INCOME...

POSTS of ANDREW L. STEVANS

1) Using a typical 25-year rank-and-file member who retired this year. The pension would be the sum of two calculations. First, multiply $172,443 [the average salary over the last three years] times 20 years times 0.017. Then, multiply $172,443 times 5 years times 0.01 and add that number to the first calculation. The total: about $67,250 per year.

2) A three-term congressman (or one-term senator) who has now reached retirement age would be eligible for an annual pension of $17,588 for six years of work. That's generous, but not close to full pay.
NOTE: Snopes.com and FactCheck.org have debunked the claim that members of Congress don't pay into their Social Security (they have since 1984) or that they don't contribute anything toward their retirement (they do).

MEDICAL BENEFITS... (Federal Employee Benefits Program) *Senators and congressmen have the same benefits pool to choose from as other federal workers.*

THINKING IN PRIVATE… The Present, Past and Future

On Aug. 11, 2009, an audience member asked President Barack Obama why members of Congress have a different health care plan than the rest of us.

Obama answered, "Their deal is no better than the janitor that cleans their offices because they are part of a federal employee plan. It is a huge pool. You've got millions of people who are part of the pool which means they have enormous leverage with the insurance companies. ... That drives down their costs, and they get a better deal."

We should note that while janitors and members of Congress can choose from the same menu of plans, members of Congress generally have more money to spend on, well, anything. Many members of Congress are millionaires.

But Obama is right that lawmakers and janitors are eligible for the same benefits, deductibles and co-pays.

SOURCES: The non-partisan Congressional Research Service, Politifact.com, FactCheck.org and Snopes.com

POSTS of ANDREW L. STEVANS

Decision-Making under Stress

Two Approaches examined...

TWO INDIVIDUALS have an identical problem. Their employer has become watchful of employee conduct. Their department has had recent firings for incompetence. Management has just discovered a serious error and the finger is starting to point.....

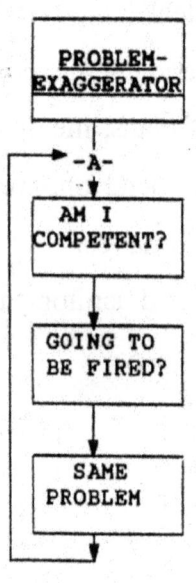

YES, BUT IT'S HOPELESS. THEIR MINDS ARE MADE UP!"

"YES, I'VE FAILED; AND I WON'T FIND ANOTHER JOB!"

"I CAN'T DO ANYTHING RIGHT! WHY IS THIS HAPPENING TO ME?!" (THE PROBLEM EXAGGERATOR RETURNS TO STEP -A-, THUS GOING INTO A CONTINUOUS, INESCAPABLE LOOP.)

THINKING IN PRIVATE... The Present, Past and Future

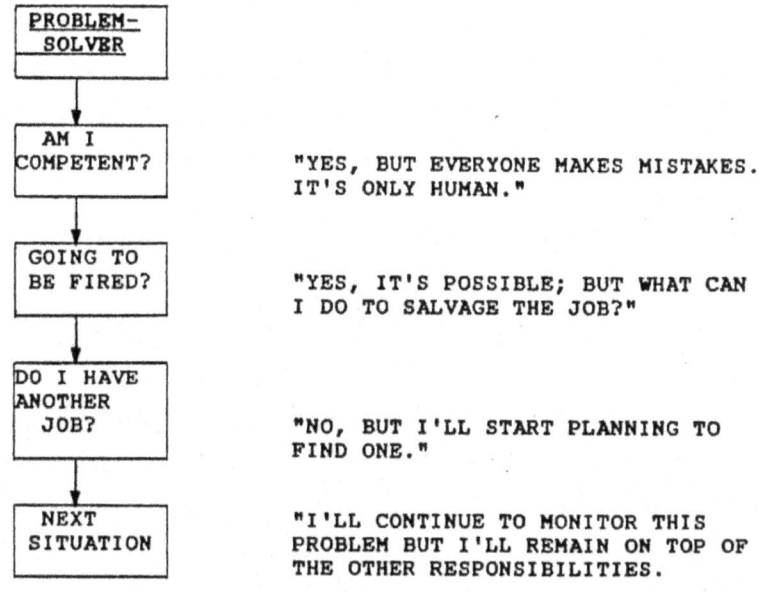

The two logic flows, above, makes an interesting point. The problem-exaggerator is paralyzed with his problem. According to the experts, his adrenalin is pumping and he is regressing into the "fight or flight" mode or what psychologists call the General Adaptation Syndrome. In reality, the problem exaggerator is no longer able to focus on the solution because of his stress reaction. Instead, he's working on a full blown anxiety attack. The problem has become secondary.

Bruce McEwen, a neuroscientist at Rockefeller University in New York and the author of *The End of Stress as We Know It* explains the serious side effects of stress. "The

POSTS of ANDREW L. STEVANS

human body reacts to stress by first pumping adrenaline and then cortisol into the bloodstream to focus the mind and body for immediate action — a response that has ensured our survival over the millennia. Generally considered a bad stress hormone, cortisol does serve many important functions — one of which is turning off inflammation. But when chronic stress exposes the body to a relentless stream of cortisol, as happens when stress is constant, cells become desensitized to the hormone, "causing inflammation to go wild," Cohen says. Long-term chronic inflammation damages blood vessels and brain cells, leads to insulin resistance (a precursor to diabetes) and promotes painful joint diseases.

It is recognized that many of us become subjective and unfocused, initially, during stressful times. A solution is to develop a giving nature, to relax between stressful situations and to accept ourselves as imperfect and "only human". This may help to alleviate much of the pressures of day-to-day life.

Establishing realistic objectives and performing careful planning provides an orderly and less stressful life. We learn to perform within the framework of our own drives and ambitions, thus achieving our objectives in a timely and less stressful manner.

"Stress is a major part of living. It is the great equalizer." **Ann Landers**

Excerpt: **PPM: Planning & Personal Marketing,** Andrew L. Stevans

THINKING IN PRIVATE... The Present, Past and Future

Predicting Long-Term Success
Assessing a Job Applicant's Soft Skills

DO YOU WANT TO HIRE AN EXECUTIVE who's a marketing genius but unbearably arrogant, or an employee who's a whiz at software but a social misfit? Assessing *soft skills*, lately called the *"Behavioral Interview"* is an important part of the hiring process once a technically qualified candidate is found.

STARBUCKS' APPROACH TO ASSESSING SOFT SKILLS... Christine Deputy, a regional director of human resources for Starbucks Coffee, using focus groups and interviews with top store managers, developed specific sets of questions to elicit evidence of past competencies.

Like Starbucks, other employers are no longer asking candidates, "What would you do if 'X' happened?" Instead, they focus on uncovering behaviors already used by the candidate in earlier work situations. Employers are now asking candidates to describe a time when they demonstrated specific needed behavior.

Candidates are asked a three-part question: 1) to summarize a situation, 2) To describe their approach in resolving the situation, and 3) to share the final outcome. "If they cannot tell a story, if they cannot answer "how" they resolved a situation, they do not have the competency," says Deputy.

ASKING THE RIGHT QUESTIONS... A common mistake interviewers make is to ask theoretical, future-oriented questions. The questions are presented as "What would you do if..." This approach allows the candidate to respond with what *he feels* the hiring manager wants to hear.

Isn't it more valuable to know how an applicant has solved work situations in the past? The responses can then be used as a predictor of what can be expected in the future.

Gary Cluff, an HR consultant and founder of No. Virginia's *Project SAVE* provides examples of the type of questions to ask a candidate in order to assess their soft skills. The answers will help predict the applicant's future success.

THINKING IN PRIVATE... The Present, Past and Future

-- Can you tell me about a mistake you made once that taught you a career lesson? What prompted you to respond that way?

-- Tell me about a time when you had to deal with an uncooperative group or team member. How did you handle it?

--Talk me through a recent project you worked on. What was your role? What problems did you encounter? How did you resolve them? What were the final results?

--Think of a time when you were under a lot of pressure at work. What were the circumstances? What did you do? How did it turn out?

--We all have had times when we haven't been pleased with our performance. Tell me about a time when this happened to you. How has your behavior changed as a result?

It's important to know what an individual has achieved in the past. What is just as important is how they did it. Learning the "how" can predict not only future performance on the job, but also the long-term success of an otherwise qualified candidate.

The father of success is work, the mother of achievement is ambition. **anon**

POSTS of ANDREW L. STEVANS

High Performance Cultures:
Best Company/Best Employer Secret Revealed

BY USING COMPETENCIES AND CULTURE in a proper way, organizations are able to build high performing talent geared to the organization's goals.

Competencies and Culture are often confused since both manifest themselves in behaviors. One difference is that most *competencies* imply a learned skill, for example, computer programming, while *cultural values* are personal characteristics, such as showing respect for others (see earlier article: *Behavior 101*) or contributing to the esprit de corp.

PM: PERFORMANCE MANAGEMENT emerges... Since the 1980's, numerous studies have attempted to discover an equation that defined a *Best Company/Best Employer*

THINKING IN PRIVATE... The Present, Past and Future

profile. One thing was certain: regardless of company size or industry, those organizations with formal Performance Management (PM) processes reflected a cultural environment where customers and employees were treated equally.

In the early 1990's, it was proven beyond any reasonable doubt that companies with a formal PM process had greater profits, better cash flows, stronger market performance and higher stock values than those without PM.

The definition of a PM process is fairly straight forward and can be explained from three perspectives: CUSTOMERS: satisfy the employees so they will satisfy the customers; pick people with a service mindset, and promote service as the highest order activity. EMPLOYEES: motivate employees to play by the rules, management must measure selectively and reward what they measure in order to build a continuous-improvement environment. PRODUCTS: remove organizational barriers to creativity, for example, do not distract people with HR concerns or with other unnecessary organizational concerns, and do not differentiate rewards (similar value) in the organization.

POSTS of ANDREW L. STEVANS

Over the past few years, studies have produced an equation that reflects a Best Company/Best Employer profile: EXECUTIVE COMMITMENT: belief in their people + EMPLOYEE ATTITUDE: highly engaged, committed employees + PEOPLE PRACTICES: mutual respect among employees and the customer = BEST COMPANY/BEST EMPLOYER. In this environment employees understand and like "the deal" and focus on doing whatever it takes to deliver superior business results.

In summary, a high performance cultural environment relies on talent. To build talent you must have employees with high-performance competencies and strong cultural values.

The Talent Solution, **Gubman, Edward L.** McGraw Hill, 2009, AMA

THINKING IN PRIVATE... The Present, Past and Future

Cultural Hegemony

The Weakening of the American Dream

WHEN A COMPLEX SUBJECT of great national concern requires explanation, it is sometimes best to quote or paraphrase exceptional writers who have shown their concern over the same subject. Studs Turkel refers to cultural hegemony as a clouding-over of our (America's) native intelligence by political leaders.

One recent political initiative, the renewed Star Wars initiative, was promoted in order to maintain a large military cold-war budget. During the George W. Bush administration, there were political manipulations that went well beyond the H. W. Bush years. The effort involved "filtering up" to the very rich much of our current budget surplus. Then there is the on-going Social Security scare that shouldn't ever have been.

POSTS of ANDREW L. STEVANS

We are seeing immense and costly negative political manipulations attempting to "un-legislate" Obamacare (aka: The Affordable Care Act), a US law aimed at reforming the American health care system and providing more Americans with access to affordable health insurance, improving the quality of health care and health insurance, regulating the health insurance industry, and reducing health care spending in the US. A big but necessary bill, placed into law for the common man, approved by the highest court in the land--but undermining the special interests of the super almighty rich, their lobbyists and their congressional partners.

A major part of the problem, one that gives the corporate wealthy and their lackeys in the congress their bite, is an apathy among the general population to become involved in local politics. We do not turn out in large numbers when voting for elected officials. We do not attend (town meetings) and discuss the topics of concern with politicians running for elected office. According to Turkel, this is at the core of the problem—and his original comment was made in 1970. Times haven't changed.

THINKING IN PRIVATE... The Present, Past and Future

In 2008 Susan Jacoby, writing for the Washington Post, commented, "The mind of this country, taught to aim at low objects, eats upon itself". Ralph Waldo Emerson offered that observation in 1837, but his words echo with painful prescience in today's very different United States. "Americans are in serious intellectual trouble -- in danger of losing our hard-won cultural capital to a virulent mixture of anti-intellectualism, anti-rationalism and low expectations."

In Steve Allan's book "Vulgarians at the gate," one of several of Allan's books on the "Dumbing of America" he makes a summary observation:

"The question is: What kind of a society will we bequeath to our children. Will it be a society dominated by media conglomerates that push anything for a quick buck, or one that reflects the highest standards of our heritage? It's up to us to do something about it, to raise a chorus of protest that echoes the words of the TV anchorman from *Network*, 'I'm mad as hell, and I'm not going to take it anymore!'"

POSTS of ANDREW L. STEVANS

A POSITIVE NOTE ON THE (ACA) AFFORDABLE CARE ACT
There may soon be a slowdown in modern medicine's centralizing. Doctors' house calls are most likely coming back and Emergency rooms may not be nearly as full.

There are many areas of the Affordable Care Act that will have a major impact on the high price of medicine and patient care in America. ACA funded a three-year incentive program called Independence at Home. Like other cost saving experiments the ACA has set in motion, Independence at Home does not propose a new way of delivering health care—it just shows a new way of funding it.

Started in 2012, 17 participating house-call practices could expect an annual bonus based on how much money they saved Medicare by keeping patients healthy and out of the hospital. Because these house-call teams serve some of Medicare's sickest and most expensive patients, the savings have the potential to be substantial. By avoiding emergency room visits and being treated at home, the patients are healthier and the families happier. The first year's results are due out soon.
One Doctor's Economic Case for House Calls. **Jeff Guo,** the Washington Post (11-09-14),

"We have two Governments in Washington: one run by the elected people—which is a minor part—and one run by the moneyed interests, which control everything." **Studs Terkel,** 1970, "Hard Times: An Oral History of the Great Depression"

THINKING IN PRIVATE... The Present, Past and Future

Arrogance in the System

Special Interests, affluence, and the Law

Summer, 2005

PRESIDENTS COME AND PRESIDENTS GO, yet the financial, medical/pharmaceutical, petroleum lobbyists and our military elite continue to escape proper scrutiny.

A strong case in point is the medical insurers. The medical HMOs make shameless – and illegal – queries of employers who are searching for better medical insurance rates. The HMOs' message: we are for-profit, and only the healthiest are going to have insurance coverage. Then there are the hospitals where hospital accountants and insurers conduct meetings to determine how to maximize profits on sick patients. Suggestion: let's require all HMOs and PPOs to be not-for-profit with Federal and State watchdog organizations, similar to Medicare, keeping an eye on medical insurers and their cost overruns.

Before the Savings and Loan (S&L) problems of the late 1980s, a borrower could obtain a signature loan at a six percent interest rate and have a savings account earning five percent. Putting aside the excuses bandied about for the S&L crises, for example, lower inflation, deregulation, the lingering effects of the Viet Nam war, etc., etc., the consumer continues to "pay the price" enduring double-digit consumer personal-loan rates – the highest (by 100%) in history--during a long-term economic growth period. During this same time period, savings account holders have earned historical lows of less than 1% on savings interest.

Here's a snap-shot of the financial ethics disasters and divisiveness that's hurt the nation. By 1989, the estimated cost of the Savings and Loan crisis had conservatively reached $500 billion. A small cadre of individuals, benefitting from the nationwide scandal, hid their wealth. Individuals like Charles Keating and his 1986 junk-bond fraud (and the five senators who protected him), spent only four-years in jail, but his manipulations cost investors and tax payers well over three-billion dollars. Michael Milken with his insider-trading schemes during the late 1980s, spent only twenty-two months in jail, yet cost investors over one-billion dollars. An appalling side note: in 2010, Milken still had a net worth of $2.3 billion. Neil Bush and the Silverado S&L failure and his $100 million loan approval to two business friends (there were no criminal felony charges and his father's Republican friends paid off Neil Bush's $50,000 court settlement fine).

More recently, the Subprime Mortgage Crisis, a nationwide banking emergency, created the recession of December 2007 – June 2009. The cause was a banking and insurance company fiasco, where mortgage lenders were no longer required to maintain healthy reserves to back mortgage loans. Carefully crafted (then lobbied for) legislation allowed the insurance companies (AIG) to guarantee the banks' (bad) loans. Tens of thousands of low-quality subprime mortgage loans were originated.

And then there's the military's (military-industrial - political complex) attempts, since the Reagan administration, to maintain a war budget by insistent demands for funding the hugely expensive ($700 billion over 25 years) SDI: Strategic Defense (Star Wars) Initiative involving an anti-ballistic missile shield *similar to the popular science fiction films by George Lucas.* More recently, the military demanded funding of super-modern missile and jet fighter programs. Instead, our high-ranking brass should have used current funding to maintain and enhance existing weapons systems, to improve (instead of close) military bases; to increase the wages of career enlisted personnel and promote them in a far more timely manner (see post: *Military Pay*").

As an interesting aside, in past years MIT had its engineering students do a required reading of a sci-fi short story that provided a chronology of events between two warring planets. The winning planet stuck to current but updated war technology. The losing planet kept attempting to implement the latest, high-priced, new-technological weapons of mass destruction. Apparently, our military is ignoring the moral of this story.

THINKING IN PRIVATE... The Present, Past and Future

When President Johnson left office he commented that duplicity (antonym: honesty) in government ultimately will ruin the country. Today, duplicity is alive and well. In fact, it's thriving! Perhaps it always has...

"I weep for the liberty of my country when I see at this early day of its successful experiment that corruption has been imputed to many members of the House of Representatives, and the rights of the people have been bartered for promises of office." **Andrew Jackson**, U.S. president: 1829 – 1837.

POSTS of ANDREW L. STEVANS

A Belated Message to Our Congress

OVER THE YEARS several individuals and groups on the Internet have claimed credit for the following poem. In 1969, as my birthday gift, I received a plaque from my seven-year old son. It had no title, and contained no author. He had bought it for 35 cents at W.T. Grant Company, located a few blocks from our home.

The actual wording of my son's gift:
   If there is righteousness in the heart, there will be beauty in the character.
   If there is beauty in the character, there will be harmony in the home.

THINKING IN PRIVATE... The Present, Past and Future

If there is harmony in the home, there will be order in the nation.

When there is order in the nation, there will be peace in the world.

I've modified the poem to read a bit differently, in order to send a message to our stymied government leaders...

If there is righteousness in the Congress, there will be agreement in the House and the Senate.

If there is agreement in the House and Senate, there will be unity in the constituency.

If there is unity in the constituency, there will be order in the nation.

When there is order in the nation, there will be peace in the world.

Regardless of the poem's source, I think most will agree it is as applicable today as when it was written—in either form.

POSTS of ANDREW L. STEVANS

Pretense

A CHARADE, A SHAM, POSTURING, Facade, Deceit... What an ambitious word pretense is. Pretense is found in the arrogance of the schooled; in the false pride of the uneducated; in the self-righteous. It is the poor man's shield; the rich man's grace; the capitalist's religion; the vain's conceit. A refined lie is this pretense. In its least offensive form it is make-believe, a charade. In its more sadistic form it's completely disingenuous, intending to deceive. Its greatest enemies are honesty, sincerity, and truth.

Pretense is the politician's reason d'être--the forced smile, the implied patronage. It is the executive's promotional carrot--the false promises, the assured favor. There should be

THINKING IN PRIVATE... The Present, Past and Future

laws against pretense. It visits with flattery, but wastes others' most precious commodity, time.

Unlike animal stalking, pretense approaches openly, fawning beauty, but hiding an ugly face. The Beatitudes of pretense are to provide false hope to the hopeless; to replace faith with doubt; to deceive the helpless; to benefit from those in mourning; to defile the clean of heart; to take unfair advantage of the sick; to distress the merciful; to exploit the oppressed.

Pretense is the posturing of fools, ignorant of their own true natures.

"A bizarre sensation pervades a relationship of pretense. No truth seems true. A simple morning's greeting and response appear loaded with innuendo and fraught with implications. Each nicety becomes more sterile and each withdrawal more permanent." **Maya Angelou**

POSTS of ANDREW L. STEVANS

Gas Price Manipulation

A FEW YEARS BACK, well, actually, it was 1965. Gas was 35.9 cents a gallon at the pump. At the time, a question was raised, "Can't we get rid of the 9/10ths of a cent?"

As America often does with wise questions affecting most of us, a study was conducted to determine how much money the oil companies made with the 0.9 or 9/10ths of a cent tacked on the per gallon price. The results were an eye opener. With a single penny increase in the price of gasoline, extra millions of dollars flowed into the coffers of the oil companies.

Today, we're in a time when the price of gas at the pump can fluctuate by a dime, or a quarter, or fifty cents or more, in a matter of days. Billions in profits are being realized by the oil companies during these "up" periods. It's interesting that higher gas prices are occurring annually—typically during the highest consumer gas demand times—holidays and summer vacation travel times.

In March of 2012, the price of gas was $1.82 per gallon. Later in the year, the Obama administration discovered that wealthy Wall Street speculators were artificially manipulating the price of oil and thus driving up the price of gasoline at the pump.

Oil is a commodity essential to the defense of the country. Laws were quickly put in place to stop or slow the speculation. Yet, to this day, the price of gas at the pump continues to fluctuate wildly. We must ask, "Don't recent gas price fluctuations break the law?

In recent months, the price of a gallon of gasoline at the pump was $3.50 per gallon. Correction: $3.50 and 9/10 of a cent.

POSTS of ANDREW L. STEVANS

Drug Companies

Affluence and the Law: 2015

PRESCRIPTION DRUGS: For way too long, the pharmaceutical industry and their lobbyists at PHARMA have been manipulating drug costs. A case in point is the exorbitant dollar amounts claimed as expenditures for "research and development" of a new drug, when, in fact, the greed factor and advertising costs are the true reasons for much of the claimed R&D costs. These questionable charges significantly drive up the cost of drugs to the consumer. Three cases in point: Diovan, Lantus and Humalog.

NOTE: Diovan is used for blood pressure control, Lantus is the only 12 hour, long-acting insulin and Humalog is an effective short acting insulin.

DIOVAN (used to control blood pressure; Angiotensin II receptor)

THINKING IN PRIVATE... The Present, Past and Future

03-2014 **$194.27** DIOVAN 320 mg: **30 day supply**: Mfr: NOVARTIS
11-2011 **$120.54 (a 60% cost increase in less than three years)**

LANTUS (slow release--12 hour--insulin) CLAIMED MFG COST
04-2014 **$612.20** LANTUS (3 vials) **30 day supply**: Mfr: AVENTIS
12-2011 **$364.59 (a 68% cost increase in less than three years)**

HUMALOG (fast acting insulin) CLAIMED MFG COST
03-2014 **$526.17** HUMALOG (3 vials) **30 day supply**: ELI LILLY & CO
11-2011 **$364.17 (a 45% cost increase in less than three years)**

The cost increases in the above listed drugs by the wealthiest of the pharmaceutical companies are, in my opinion criminal acts against the sickest of America. Many elderly diabetics are absolutely terminal without the three listed drugs and, due to advanced illness and age, are unable to appeal or defend their medical needs. Without these medications, many advanced diabetics have developed kidney leaks and are quickly approaching the dialysis end-stage of their illness.

The solution, at least regarding the rising expense for Diovan, came as no surprise to some of us. One of the largest Plan-D Medicare prescription drug plans removed Diovan from its formulary for 2015. Other drug plans followed suite.

SOME HOPE... Of course, the direct loss would be to our diabetic patients and those needing this important medication for their blood pressure control. Fortunately, there is an inexpensive blood pressure medication currently available called Losartin. Losartin is not only a good substitute for Diovan, it has fewer side effects.

Regarding Lantus (re: the earlier chart), unfortunately, this is the only long acting (12 hour) insulin currently available. It's an interesting note that the patent on Lantus expired some time ago. Yet, either by an honest lack of an alternative, or by design, there appears to be no generic replacement for Lantus at this time. And the price keeps skyrocketing.

Note: There's a new game in town and a possible solution. It's called *pharmacogenomics*, a.k.a., "The One-Pill Solution." Using a $100 genetics test, the patient's medications are individualized in order to maximize effectiveness of drugs and minimize side effects.

"You can fool too many of the people too much of the time." **James Thurber**, 20th century American author, journalist

Medical Murder?

Psychosurgery in the 20th century

WHILE ATTENDING PENN STATE in the 1960s, I took an advanced Speech class. From a list of speaking subjects, I chose EST: Electro Shock Therapy. While researching EST, I happened upon a detailed article on the failures in Frontal Lobotomy operations. Never quite recovering from the descriptions of this horror, I realized how primitive the practice of medicine can be.

An aside: Over the past few years, some medical professionals have discussed removing the tiny area of the brain where fanaticism spawns (re: Post: *Fear Tactics—the ISMs*). Of course that same neural area contains our unique character and beliefs including our faith and hope and basic goodness, in other words our humanity.

POSTS of ANDREW L. STEVANS

Among those who study the human brain, there is a consensus that it will take many decades, possibly a hundred years or more to comprehend, in any significant detail, the whole brain's complexity. This has not stopped the medical community from playing God with an area of our brain called the Frontal Lobe.

In 1935, Dr. Egas Moniz, a Portuguese doctor, was awarded the Nobel Prize in physiology and medicine after he discovered the technique of drilling through the skull and severing the frontal lobe from the thalamus. It became known as a Frontal Lobotomy. Its suggested use was to relieve severe physical pain. This was a time before antipsychotic medication. This "practical" procedure was the only effective treatment for depression, schizophrenia, suicidal tendencies and other severe emotions and behaviors.

Starting in Washington DC, in 1946 and during the late 1940s and 50s, in the U.S. alone, 40,000 to 50,000 "ice pick" frontal lobotomies were performed. This faster procedure did not require entry through the skull. The procedure freed the

THINKING IN PRIVATE... The Present, Past and Future

medical community to do other things and freed the patient, who had often existed "institutionalized and in squalor."

It wasn't much later that frontal lobotomies were considered the cure for individuals suffering from bi-polar disorders, hyper-activity, anxiety and panic attacks, post partum melancholy—the list goes on. The Frontal Lobotomy surgical procedure, claiming to "cure the sick soul", was successful only one-third of the time. Some within our medical community, even today, do not consider killing the aspiring nature of the patient's mind as murder.

Partial source: *Psychcentral*: 2011/03/21: history-of-the-lobotomy

"You're on your own. And you know what you know. And YOU are the one who'll decide where to go..." **Theodor Geisel** (Dr. Seuss)

POSTS of ANDREW L. STEVANS

The Computer Elite

And Planned Obsolescence

SOMETIMES YOU HAVE TO WONDER: Are the Justice and Defense Departments investigating the "real" business practices of the computer giants, namely, the annual (sometimes semi-annual) new, larger and faster computers needed to run their new, time consuming, memory-eating, updated operating systems and applications software—did I mention expensive? (See endnote: "On National Systems Security." What are the national security ramifications?")

THE TREND-- The 1989's MS DOS PC operating system (an IBM/Microsoft jointly held copyright) used the government's preferred letter-writing program called "WordPerfect." At the time, the average written page required

THINKING IN PRIVATE... The Present, Past and Future

1,000 bytes (alpha or numeric characters), and was saved in one second (stored for later printing and reference) on a 7 MHz (7 million cycles per second) computer (Note: as a comparison, a light bulb blinks on and off at 60 hertz or 120 flickers per second).

In 1994, using Microsoft's new MS Windows 3.1 and Microsoft's "Word" (Microsoft letter-writing software), an average written page required 11,000 bytes and was saved on a 125 Mhz PC in 10 seconds.

In 1997, using Microsoft's new Windows 98 and Microsoft's Word, the average written page required 21,000 bytes and was saved on the same computer or PC in as much as 20 seconds. Today, Microsoft no longer supports Windows 98, nor the next generation called Windows XP. And the computer speeds have increased many fold, going from Mhz (millions of cycles per second), to Ghz (billions of cycles per second). A conciliatory note: Today, one typewritten page requires only 17,000 bytes—and Windows 7 stores it in a second or two. Thank you, thank you, Microsoft!

POSTS of ANDREW L. STEVANS

THE TIMING of the latest release: Many individuals and corporations are barely able to keep up with all of the updates and additions incorporated into the latest releases of Microsoft's Windows 7, and now, lo and behold, there's Windows 8 and 8.1. And we've just been informed that Windows 9 is on the horizon because of the glitches in Windows 8 (or is it 8.1?). I'm informed Microsoft skipped Windows 9 (abandoned?). So, now, the coming release will be Windows 10. I'm sure you can find advance pricing and the latest release date for Windows 10 on the Internet.

A question that begs an answer is: Why aren't the latest Windows releases, that contain admitted "patches" to errors causing confusion in users in earlier releases, FREE, like the recalls by the auto manufacturers? Another question: Will these latest software releases also lose Microsoft's support in the near future? I think the answer is YES—of course!

It's difficult to lend much if any credibility to past statements made by large computer company executives, all having realized immense personal wealth overcharging for their latest computers and related software over the years. But,

THINKING IN PRIVATE... The Present, Past and Future

there was an encouraging remark made in 1999 that appeared to carry with it a promise. The comment was credited to Salesforce.com's CEO Marc Benioff or Oracle's CEO, Larry Ellison, depending on who you talk to,

Soon, it was claimed, by using Internet software, any computer, regardless of speed or current electronics, will run any software, whether it is a word processor, spread sheet, presentation software or other applications software--at equal speeds and of equal quality. Note that nowhere in this comment is mentioned the word FREE!"

Yet, today, it appears we continue to require frequent investments in new PC upgrades in order to run the even more time and space consuming, expensive versions of Microsoft's WORD, Microsoft's Office and the myriad of other expensive Microsoft software required to be purchased by every individual, business and government in the civilized world.

Though we shouldn't hold our collective breaths, the current understanding is that the upcoming new internet software, hinted at earlier, will be public domain, and with free downloads.

POSTS of ANDREW L. STEVANS

Public Domain? Is this the "Cloud" that now resides in the Internet's ionosphere? It's surprising how quickly this relatively new concept quietly took hold, and not too long ago. Amazon launched its cloud-based services back in 2002! According to Michael Skok, a general partner at North Bridge Venture Partners, an investment company that conducts the annual cloud-computing survey, "Today, cloud-computing powers online banking and shopping email programs such as Gmail and Yahoo, social networks, online photo and music storage, and digital libraries such as Netflix and Kindle."

Still, it appears the Federal government, as well as major corporate hardware and software lobbyists and their related special interests, hold the reins regarding continued maintenance of older software releases, new software, the latest hardware--and fair play. For example, as of April, 2015, Microsoft's Windows XP will no longer be maintained nor will it receive security updates--for non-government users.

Lately, I've heard talk that we should pin our hopes on established UNIX-based PC operating system software. (UNIX software is often found hard-wired into smart phones, computer tablets, routers and video games.) UNIX software is

THINKING IN PRIVATE… The Present, Past and Future

FREE for computer users and has an open source operating system appropriately named "LINUX rising." Steve Wozniak made the comment, "I've never met a LINUX user that I didn't like."

"All my life I wanted to be part of a revolution. My donation was from the technology side. The companies, the rich people—they had control of the computers. We were going to take it away from them."
Steve Wozniak, cofounder of Apple Computer.

A Note on National Systems Security… As a working society, we are kept busy purchasing and attempting to understand the latest software; and how to make it run on the required faster computers. The ongoing question of all users is "How do we now achieve "our" requirements using "their" latest operating systems and applications software." At the same time, the super-rich computer elite are busy developing and feeding us expensive new hardware and software operating systems (now, Windows 10)--and their other latest electronic toys, meanwhile ignoring their obligation to the nations: to make their computer systems secure, and to invest their money and research today, to harden our communications and infrastructure, now.

In late October 2014, Joel Brenner, a former Inspector general and senior counsel of the National Security Agency said in his Washington Post article, *Virtual Networks, real-life enemies,* "When a device is connected to an electronic network, it can be disabled or destroyed through commands issued on that network. This applies to missile launchers, railway switches, manufacturing tools and any other computer driven machine." Recently the Pentagon announced that it is pushing for construction of its own power grids at bases around the country. Is this just another military-Industrial boondoggle? What about our country's security? What about us? In this urgent regard, we have a long way to go before we sleep.

POSTS of ANDREW L. STEVANS

"SILENCE IS THE GREAT ENEMY OF FREEDOM"
anon

"Those who sacrifice essential liberties for the sake of temporary freedom deserve neither liberty nor freedom."

Benjamin Franklin

www.ingramcontent.com/pod-product-compliance
Lightning Source LLC
Chambersburg PA
CBHW071450040426
42444CB00008B/1280